To Willie

From Father Thornton

Xmas 1920

G.

TWENTY-THREE YEARS A MISSIONER.

TWENTY-THREE YEARS A MISSIONER.

LIFE-SKETCH LESSONS AND REMINISCENCES.

BY

Rev. THOMAS WAUGH.

Third Edition 16,000.

LONDON:
CHARLES H. KELLY, 2, CASTLE STREET, CITY ROAD, E.C.
ROCHDALE:
JOYFUL NEWS BOOK DEPOT, 70, DRAKE STREET.

Dedication.

To my beloved daughter, Ruby S. Waugh,
with my earnest prayers for
her future witness and work for Christ.

PREFACE.

As the early part of this volume is really a brief autobiography, and the remainder a history of my own life-work with lessons suggested by it, I have consented to write it, with great diffidence, and only in response to long, multiplied, and oft-repeated requests. I have told "the story of my conversion" at least 250 times in this land, and God has made it the means of leading thousands of people, specially young men, to the Saviour. Hundreds of Christians have urged me to print it, and to add something about my early life, my local preacher and college days, and about my life-work and its most helpful lessons and incidents.

Because one naturally shrinks from writing about one's own life-setting and toil I have resisted many urgent appeals for long years, but have at last consented to write and publish. If this volume be *of God*, then it is certainly *opportune*, for the *revival note* is, in these latter days, growing in power and clearness and spreading from church to church and from district to district in a delightful fashion. The spiritual sky is laden with heavy clouds charged with "showers of blessing." When the Christian church's fitness for use, her spirit of intercession, of willingness to toil and sacrifice, and of sympathy with perishing men, shall have risen to the will of God, the higher gravitation will grip these heavenly clouds of Divine power and grace, and give us mighty revival of spiritual religion—the nation's first and greatest need. The revival hunger is deepening in the hearts of scores of young ministers and laymen; and letters are constantly reaching me asking for counsel, lessons, and help in winning men to God.

It is because of these things that this volume appears at this time instead of being left to an eventide, if there should be one in my life. By special request, I have here repeated, but more fully, three or four of the special illustrations of answered prayer that have appeared in two of my previous volumes. They have been specially asked for because God has specially blessed them to a large number of readers.

That at "such a time as this," the Lord, who has condescended to bless my voice and pen in the past, may make this volume a messenger of help and blessing, for His own glory, is my supreme object and prayer in its issue to the world.

THOMAS WAUGH.

71, Avondale Road,
Southport.

CONTENTS.

ILLUSTRATIONS.

TWENTY-THREE YEARS A MISSIONER.

CHAPTER I.

My Early Home Life.

I WAS born on September 3rd, 1853, at Quarry Beck, near Brampton, in Cumberland, and few people have started life in a bonnier place. The quaint old cottage is on three sides surrounded by noble trees, and on two sides its fine garden is bounded by a lovely trout stream. It stands at the western entrance to Naworth Park, and is one mile from Naworth Castle, the seat of the Earl and Countess of Carlisle. It is also just one mile from the fine old Priory at Lanercost, and two miles from the south-western point of the Roman wall. The neighbourhood was the scene of stirring and tragic incidents in the old days of border forays and warfare.

My mother was born in the same cottage, and her mother went to it when six years of age. Being one of the older members of a large family, and her mother having been left a widow a few years previously, my mother was sorely needed in the old home. Consequently she and my father made this their home for some three years after their marriage, and only left it for Cummersdale, near Carlisle, when I was nearly two years old. My father had previously left the flour mill near Brampton, where he had been for several years, to take charge of a larger mill near our new home. He managed that mill and we lived in Cummersdale until I was seven and a half years of age.

Before I was six years old my father at nights taught me the rudiments of education, and did much to develop in me a good memory by making me learn and remember a great deal of poetry. To that initial home training I owe very much to this day. There I went to school with dear old Mr. Morrison, who was afterwards drowned in the dark, in the river Caldew that flows past the village. He must have noticed that I had a good memory, also that I had a terrible tendency *to talk*, for he often said to me, "Tom, you will be a bishop some day!" Knowing nothing of Nonconformity, all his ideas of the ministry were necessarily Anglican, yet his prophecy has had some fulfilment.

In those early days I had the beginnings of my present passion for *reading*. I fear that when not thus employed nor asleep I was very noisy, and many a penny I have received if I would sit down and be still for an hour. I could only do this when I had a book to read, and those pennies were the first moneys I received through books. When ten years of age I had read practically everything in my father's little library, and everything I could borrow. Much of it no doubt was rubbish, but much also has been useful to me ever since. In those boyhood days I devoured "The Life and Works of Lord Byron"; the histories of Rome and Greece, "The Punic Wars," "The Conquest of Peru," and that of Mexico, and also the works of Goldsmith. For such I am to-day devoutly thankful, for it has been useful to me ever since.

In February 1861 we went to live at Allerby Mill, near Maryport in West Cumberland, and my people were there for twenty-four years. Soon after our arrival I began to attend the village school at Gilcrux nearly a mile and a half away. After the first year my schooling was terribly interrupted, as, beginning in the April before I was nine years of age to work on the farm, during the spring, summer, and autumn months, I for three years only got to school for a few months in the winter. We had gone to the mill and farm from a cottage, and in making his way my father had to begin at the bottom. As a result we all had to work as soon as we were at all equal to it. In early spring the land had to be cleaned and prepared for the green crops, and the stones to be gathered from the fields intended for hay. Then the potatoes were to plant; and, later, they and the turnips were to hoe and clean, and the thistles and ragwort had to be cut down in the pastures.

The flour mill too provided work for me as well as for my father and the miller. I had to go out and deliver the smaller sacks all over the neighbourhood when quite a lad, often getting back late at nights. The mill necessitated keeping day book and ledger. Of these I took charge at the age of ten, and kept them until I left home for the Christian ministry. Even in the evenings,—when not doing up the books,—horses, cattle, calves, and pigs were to feed and bed up for the night. The eggs were to be got in from the nests and the poultry made safe for the night. We had plenty to eat and plenty to wear, and even when but children we had plenty of hard work to do, if not quite enough to keep some of us out of mischief. Yes, and *hardship* too, as well as hard work. Many a keen frosty morning found my sister, my brother, and me in a field, pulling and cutting turnips with snow and frost on the leaves. Many a time the intense cold made our fingers tingle with pain till the tears would come. When but ten, eight, and seven years of age, I have known us with three horses and carts filling and leading turnips from the frozen field, at Martinmas, when the servants were away. As with the cutting, when the cold-pain got bad we used to beat our hands on our sides, blow on our fingers or put them in our mouths, do our little cry, and then go on again with the work. We never tried to shirk it; for the dear father and mother were working like slaves, and we knew we must bear our part.

We were often told that it was good for us and would help to make us hardy and brave. I could never see that, but would have liked my good to come in some other way. I am not sorry now for the toil and roughing it in those early years; but I am indeed thankful that my children have started life under easier and happier conditions. Indeed, the pendulum is in danger of swinging too far in the other direction in these days. Child-life among the upper and middle classes is so jealously guarded, and its happiness so sedulously sought, that there is the peril that the young folks may in some cases become selfish, and never learn to "endure" any "hardness" or discipline to help them through the coming battle of life.

At the age of twelve I was sent for five quarters to a Grammar School at Brampton, and during that time lived with my grandmother and aunt. That was my very best educational chance, and I worked very hard to make the most of it. I began in the fifth class and finished in the first in everything. I took certificates in every subject except two:—*conduct* and *writing*. In these I failed completely. Why I failed in the former, I fancy my family and friends understood perfectly. Why I failed in the latter, I fear my correspondents in these days understand equally well. In school or out of it, if awake my tongue would go, and at school it often got me into trouble; and I fear its cure is not yet complete. As to writing, well, my friends often ask me to read letters for them that I sent weeks or months before, and sometimes I am nearly beaten. There has been a suggestion that part of the educational portion of the Million Fund be spent on typewriters for a number of ministers, of whom I am one.

On leaving the Grammar School, my life-work had to be settled. A draper in Maryport wanted me to be apprenticed to the business; my parents inclined to it, but I did not. After some discussion I went for a month on trial, to see how I liked it. When I got home on the fourth Saturday night my father said, "What has it to be, Tom? farmer or draper?" I immediately replied; "farmer," and began at once to work on our own farm and sometimes in the mill.

I was fond of horses and cattle, and dearly loved the farm work of the next few years. To such work in such a district I owe much of the health and strength that have carried me through the strain of the last twenty-five years. In those years I built up a constitution that has stood me in splendid stead all through my ministry. From the hill behind my home we could see Skiddaw, Blencathra, Grassmoor, and others of the more northern Cumberland mountains. From the hill in front of the house and behind the opposite Coalpit we could see the gleaming waters of the Solway and the Dumfriesshire and Wigtownshire hills beyond. The blending of sea and mountain air was keen and bracing, and one of our most constant companions was a good appetite. As my parents always kept a good table and we young folks a good preparation for it, the big kitchen witnessed four times a day such a fitness of things that for twenty-four years a doctor was hardly ever on the premises.

In spring, summer, and autumn I was in the fields nearly all the day long, with the pure air going through my lungs, the sweet smell of the soil in my nostrils, the music of the birds in my ears, and never a care worth the mentioning. It had its drawbacks like all life-spheres, but it was grand! Sometimes in these latter days,—when thinking and feeling about the awful problems that lie so heavy upon the heart of church and nation; when fighting hard with the evils that curse one's fellow-men in such multitudes; when, having pleaded with men almost unto tears on Christ's behalf and their own, and perhaps, with many, pleaded in vain; or when going to face the crowd with a message from God, and almost trembling with a sense of the responsibility,—I am tempted to wish I was back in the old life, narrow and hard as it was. The thoughts swing back to bonnie spring mornings when, on the horse's back on the way to the plough, or between its handles, I was mostly without care of the world's big problems and almost without knowledge of its awful pain: mountains in front of me and mountains behind me standing out clear and sun-tipped against the heavens; the air as pure and sweet as God made it; every blade in the sprouting corn-fields carrying a dewdrop that glittered like a diamond in the light of the rising sun; and hedgerows and trees turned into a lovely orchestra by the songs of the birds. A few weeks later, and Nature donned her garb of glorious green and hid the homes of the birds whose love had led to the joys of nesting and to family cares. Then, later still, the hedgerows whitened into miles of sweet smelling May-blossom, broken with the yellow and pink of the honeysuckle and the wild rose. Later again, and the crops in the fields rose in glad repayment of the farmer's toil and care. The tubers and bulbs of the green crops swelled and grew, the hay ripened for scythe or machine, the corn whitened for the coming harvest, and the cattle and sheep fed or rested in the green pastures. They were merry happy days those, and sweeter still when I had found my Lord, and the songs and tunes I sang and whistled the day long were those of Zion. They were happy days those, when I made and prayed over my sermons at the plough or on the roads with the carts, and then walked on Sunday to preach them in town or village to the people who had known me in my sins.

But I know that life was not the best or richest life, near as it was to Nature's heart. I know that the longings for it are temptations to cowardice and ease, and, indulged in, would be sin. Even when pure and simple, much of the happiness of those days was but the happiness of carelessness and thoughtlessness, which can never be so deep and rich as that which is sanctified by sacrifice and burden-bearing. There is no joy so deep and full as that which can be touched to tears. I am thankful I had that life, though I am ashamed of the follies and sins that marred it. It was a rare chance for growing a strong body, and a fine education of the future. But I am also glad that, with all its burden of pain and tears, I was called to the thick of the battle against sin and to the heart of the great effort to win humanity to God. I am more grateful to God than I can express for my call to toil among the masses of my fellow-men and women, and to have some part in the 'filling up of that which is lacking in the afflictions of Christ' among them in trying to save some. As one sees their sins and the awful results that follow; as one sees the temptations and difficulties they have to face; as one sees the conditions that are nearly all against their reaching pure and noble manhood and womanhood—one's faith and hope are sorely tried. The burden of it all is very heavy, and the heartache of it is often unto tears. Hundreds of times I have prayed for and then pleaded with the crowd for Christ till my very life seemed to be left with them and I could hardly crawl to bed. Yet this share in the passion of Christ and the pain of the world is a wondrous honour and joy. It is helping to bear His cross, to further His purposes, to crown His mission, and to hasten His coming as earth's King. With all its toil and pain there are heights and depths of holy gladness in it, that were impossible in my free and careless farm life, even after I was a saved man.

There was one great mistake in those years of my life from sixteen to twenty-two that I now deeply regret. From the time I was sixteen I was not only doing all a man's heaviest work on the farm, but in connection with the mill I was constantly handling twenty-one-stone sacks of grain and twenty-stone sacks of flour. It is nearly always a misfortune for a lad to be big for his years, where there is a surfeit of hard work. He is almost sure to get more than his share. At seventeen I was nearly six feet in height, but I was very thin and unset, and the heavy lifting and carrying twenty-stone sacks up many stairs put a strain on me to which my physique was not quite equal. In the strain of such work I sprained some of the muscles of my heart, and thus laid the foundation for the heart collapse that overtook me in September 1894 and necessitated my resting nearly all the summer of 1895.

As I understood none of these things at the time, I made the mischief worse by my own follies. Like many men who are physically strong, I was foolishly vain of my strength. In this I was not alone, and with others often spent an hour or two in muscular competitions, especially in lifting and putting heavy weights. Even in my work among sacks of grain I often attempted and performed physical feats that were as foolhardy as they were unnecessary. For the folly of those days I am paying the price now: while still healthy and strong, I have never since 1894 been the man I was before, or been equal to the work I put in before; for the rest of my days I know I have a weakened heart, and must walk and work in harmony with that knowledge.

The religious history of my early life will form the subject of the next chapter, but one other feature of these years I sincerely regret. While I was still reading practically everything within my reach, everything scholastic was foolishly allowed to drop. Without thinking of it, I acted in harmony with the stupid idea that one's education is "finished" when one leaves school. For this mistake I had to pay a heavy price when my eyes were opened at my conversion. I had a long educational leeway to make up, which added a heavy burden to my work as a candidate for the ministry and as a student in college, and which puts limitations upon my work for God and men even now.

To the youths and maidens who read these lines I offer a piece of advice that I have acquired in the school of hard experience. While not giving up your games and recreations, or becoming old before your time, if you mean to play a man's or woman's part for God and men, and to make the most and best of your life-chance, keep up the essential lines of your studies at school. Keep them up as mental discipline, and as machinery and tools for future service. Adding to this a more advanced and wider outlook, and a deeper and wider reading, you will be intellectually ready when your Lord calls you to a fuller service in a larger sphere. You will thus be spared the long re-study of elementaries that I had to face at my conversion, and its inroads upon my limited time. For at least six years I had to spend upon the first principles of scholarship, precious time and power that should have been given to the more advanced study and reading that should, if possible, form a part of every Christian worker's equipment for service.

CHAPTER II.

My Early Religious Life.

STRICTLY speaking, this chapter is the story of my early life in relation to religion, for I had no religion at all until I reached my twenty-third year. My parents were both brought up in some slight touch with the Presbyterian Church of England. They were both strictly upright and moral, and scorned anything mean and unworthy. My mother too, when we children were growing up, often spoke to us on behalf of God and nominal religion. But neither knew anything of personal saving fellowship with Christ until their later years. As a result, while their words to us on such subjects were ever in the direction of morality and the outward form of Christianity, they knew nothing of intercession for us, and were unable to lead us to the Saviour to whom they themselves were then strangers. I write these things in all love and tenderness, for they have been good parents to us all, as far as they knew how and had the power. Thank God! they now know Christ as their own personal Saviour.

While living at Cummersdale, my father often took me to Holme Head Anglican church on Sunday mornings. In connection with that communion I had already been baptised and years afterwards underwent the rite of confirmation. When we got to Allerby Mill, where my father was for the first time in business for himself, attendance at a place of worship practically ceased for him and my mother. For the first years it was a hard uphill fight to feel his feet under him and lay a foundation for the future. Then about a farmyard, with its stock and poultry with all their calls and needs, it takes, under adverse conditions, either a very decided conviction or a definite saved experience to keep to a regular attendance upon the house of God; and the difficulty is all the greater if there be, as in our case, a rapidly increasing family of children.

And the conditions were adverse indeed. The church at Gilcrux was the nearest one, and the other two within reach were nearly two miles distant. In each case the clergyman then in charge was of the old school, which has now happily died out. They were all more at home in a public-house than fit for work in God's house, and knew much more about whisky than about the gospel of Christ. One result was that except for the gleams of light coming from a few small Congregational and Primitive Methodist chapels, the whole neighbourhood for miles around lay in dense spiritual darkness.

Though my parents almost entirely gave up attending a place of worship, they did not wish their children to be brought up like heathen; so my sister, eldest brother and I were sent most Sundays to the church at Gilcrux and to the sabbath-school connected with it. Very few adults went to church, nor can we wonder. The drunkenness of the vicar was a public scandal and source of mocking laughter, and the churchwardens were of the same type. I seriously question if there was a single person connected with the place who knew anything of a personal salvation.

There was no other place of worship in the village. The Primitive Methodists had tried again and again to get a footing in the village, and had always been driven away. June after June, at the quarterly meetings, the Maryport Wesleyans would ask; "Shall we have another try to reach and start a cause in godless Gilcrux?" But every effort for years ended in failure and defeat.

The spiritual state of the neighbourhood was simply appalling. In those days at the mining village of Bullgill, just by my father's farm, and in the mining hamlets around, nearly every man used to bet and gamble, nearly every man was more or less fond of drink, and few girls reached womanhood without losing their purity and honour. Small wonder that Bullgill was often called Sodom and the next hamlet Gomorrah. During the years of my boyhood and early manhood the usual Sunday morning programme among the men and lads was dog-racing, foot-racing, wrestling, pole-leaping, quoit-pitching, card-playing, and pitch-and-toss. On scores of Sundays I have, with others, played pitch-and-toss till noon, gone home to dinner, and then back to the gaming till tea-time. No one there dreamed of going to church except the landlord of the beershop, who went a few times each year before Brewster Sessions; and it was well known that he went then to get the vicar to use his influence in aiding him to secure a spirit licence for the house.

When nine years of age, one of our maid-servants, now a Christian worker in Manchester, took me on three consecutive Sunday afternoons to a cottage prayer-meeting arranged by two or three Primitive Methodists. Some of the hymns and tunes then sung, and some of the impressions then made upon me, never left me. I believe that those spiritual influences lived with me through the dark and sinful years that followed, and partly accounted for my ready response to the gospel when I came under its power in my manhood. I believe most firmly that, had any saved person then taken me by the hand, I should have been a saved lad from that time. Strange coincidence and beautiful reward for that unsaved village maiden for taking me to those meetings! but, more than twenty-five years later, I had the joy of leading her and her husband to Christ at Eccles.

When about twelve years old I saw that the religion at our church was a hollow sham. I had nothing real to look to, and so foolishly concluded that religion was all a sham—the first great mistake of my life. I am sorry to have to say that I never again entered a house of God to worship until I was a man in my twenty-third year. An old man living near to us took me and a few more lads under his influence, and completely upset any helpful views we had of the Christian religion. We soon adopted his oft-repeated opinion that it was an "old Oriental and worn-out superstition, got up and kept up by priests for their own comfort and ease." From that time, most healthy restraints were thrown off, and, like those around me, I greedily sought the pleasures of the world and sin.

For long years my father's father had been a drunkard, and his conduct shortened the days of my grandmother, scattered the children, and wrecked the home. My father never forgot the hardship and miseries of those years, and a hatred of drunkenness was born of it, that never left him. Thus in my early years, while drunkenness was rampant around me, I constantly heard of its dread consequences, from the experience and lips of my father, and I determined that I would never be a drunkard. When I, at ten years of age, expressed that resolve to my grandfather, he told me that, if I kept to it, I would be the first Thomas Waugh in the family as far back as he could remember, who had not been a drunkard. Thank God! The horrible entail has been broken at last, and my grandfather's statement but stiffened my resolve.

When I was about seventeen, a young fellow came to us as farm servant, who was a keen gambler. He soon led me into the fascination and bonds of greyhound coursing and horse racing, and his task was not difficult. Gambling was in the very air, and in the blood of nearly every male in the district, from boyhood to gray hairs. We lads nearly all had our favourite dogs and horses, and our heroes on the path and in the boxing and wrestling ring. In our school-days we played pitch-and-toss for coppers on our way to and from school, betted pennies in the dinner hour as to who could most quickly find places on the big school maps, and enjoyed those winter evenings the best that were spent at playing cards for money. My parents sometimes played with us but never for anything more costly than nuts, but there was not enough of excitement for us lads in stakes like those.

There are few sins so awful, in their subtle way of tightening their bonds upon their victims, as the sin of gambling. Only the slave to it can understand its fever, its spell, and its ruthless sway. Before I had betted on dogs and horses for three years, it was my absorbing passion, and I used to dream of such things at night. When neither asleep nor dreaming, I have often taken my eldest brother to a picked card party. We have begun at eight, played until ten, got hot, doubled the stakes, and never left the table till four the next morning. My father often told me that I was "dog mad." He was about right, and my passion for racing dogs and horses, and my wonderful knowledge and memory of so many of their achievements, earned me the local gambling name of "Bell's Life."

That kind of gambling at once led me to the public-house, as it has led multitudes both before and since then. When I began to take drink I did not care for it a bit. Before I had been drinking long the craving for it was awakened in my system. I did not forget my vow to my grandfather, nor the strong words of my father on the matter; and to save myself from going too far, I made a rule by which I determined to abide. When drinking spirits I always stopped after two glasses, when drinking beer I never took more than three glasses. It was easy to stop at first, but not so when I had been drinking three or four years. In my twenty-third year the craving had become such that I clearly saw that I must either become a drunkard or never touch the stuff at all. I thank my God for leading me to choose the latter course just before my conversion.

At eighteen I was well on the down line, and going fast. I was wonderfully kept from getting drunk and from yielding to the shameless immorality which formed so awful a part of my environment. For such preservation I take no credit; God was keeping me for the future, and for such keeping I am a grateful man this day. Every night when possible I had my two or three glasses of drink. Whenever possible I was among gamblers betting, and even when with my young farmer friends, religion was only a theme for scoffing and sneers. I was utterly sceptical, and looked upon it as a fable. When I was twenty my youngest sister was born, yet though the eldest then of the family of eight, no thoughts of my example to the rest held me in check. Pleasure was my god, and I loved it most when it was most exciting.

Wild and disobedient as I was, I had some real affection for my parents; and God used that as the means of keeping me from becoming a drunkard. I knew how terribly it would hurt them. He used an equally simple thing in keeping me from actual impurity. Fathers whose daughters had been ruined often came to me with their sorrow and sometimes with tears. I was a poor comforter, but I did resolve that no fathers or mothers should ever have such shame and pain through me. I give God all the praise for this, for though I did not then believe in Him, I feel sure that He was fulfilling in me His word to Cyrus,—"I girded thee when thou didst not know Me."

The late George Moore, our big-hearted Cumberland philanthropist, maintained a number of Scripture readers in ours and the adjoining county of Westmoreland. One of these men called William Black—now living at Brigham near Cockermouth—came to live at Gilcrux. Blessed little man! His very soul was a passion for the saving of men. He not only tramped the whole district for miles around, reading the Word and praying in the homes of the people, but he was one of the shrewdest and warmest button-holers I ever knew. Only the award-day of the Lord will be able to show how much the church of God owes to the work in that district of William Black and his good wife.

He had a service in a large room at his house, each Sunday evening. As people got converted there, others went, till there was not room to accommodate them. A chapel had now become a necessity, and a chapel they would have. A Churchman gave them the best site in the village, they began to pray and beg in real earnest, and in June 1875 they opened with great glee the Gilcrux Wesleyan chapel, and put it on the plan of the Maryport circuit.

Mr. Black was "No. 8" on the plan, and had to preach every third Sunday evening. His sermons were as black as his name. He accepted literally every Old and New Testament figure of the doom of the wicked, and he made them just flame before his hearers. He was a past-master at what was then termed "holding them over the pit." Many a time after I was saved he almost made my hair rise with his lurid pictures and terrific appeals. But God was with him, for he lived near to God. In spite of some crude, unlovely, and sometimes utterly unscriptural presentations of the claims of God and the future, he seldom preached without conversions. We young fellows, who called ourselves sceptics and fancied we possessed most of the wisdom in that neighbourhood, made great fun of all this. We nicknamed the meetings. The prayer-meeting was "a creeping night" and the class-meeting "a confessional." But the work went on till one or two turned to God who used to be with me at sports, balls, and sometimes at the theatre down at Maryport or Workington; and then I lost my temper!

One evening in the December of that year I gave a young dressmaker a ride to the railway station in my cart, and took her sewing machine. She was newly converted, full of zeal, and empty of fear. That lassie gave me one of the warmest fifteen minutes of my life. She pitched into me for my godlessness, threatened the direst consequences, and told me not to mock and scoff so much, as most likely I would get converted myself. I tried to fence her off, but it was no use, and trying to laugh it off was little more successful.

Christmas Day that year fell on a Saturday, and after spending the day out shooting, the night at cards, and the Sunday morning out shooting again, I went in the afternoon to chapel for the first time in my life. I only went to please my mother and a young fellow who was spending Christmas with us, and there was no impression made upon me; but my time was near.

In the beginning of January I had a strong

temptation to take some of my father's money for betting purposes. I was in need of money, and taking most of my father's cash and keeping his books, the thing would have been easy. But the devil outwitted himself. He came with the temptation before he got me quite low enough to accept it. He struck the iron before it was quite hot, and the recoil robbed him of a useful servant. The very thought that my drinking and betting had brought me so low, and so weakened my moral fibre, that I could be thus tempted, fairly shocked me and led me to serious thinking. I at once resolved on reformation, and decided to become an abstainer and to stop betting. Before the week was out I discovered that reformation cannot save a man from sin, only regeneration. Before the week was out I was back at the drink and the betting, and on the Sunday I was disgusted at my weakness and thoroughly ashamed of myself.

I felt then that I needed a power higher than my own to arrest my moral drift, and decided to go to the chapel at night, thinking I might hear something about strength or manliness. I heard Mr. Black preach on "Jesus of Nazareth passeth by," and was much impressed by the service. Without saying a word to any one I went and began a quiet perusal of the New Testament to see what this Jesus had to say for Himself. That reading of the word of God did more than all else to shatter my scepticism and to lead me to God. I went to chapel the next Sabbath evening, and on the following Saturday night, at a temperance meeting in the chapel, I, with fifteen other young men, signed the total abstinence pledge.

The next night I was again at chapel, and left it under deep conviction of sin and need. Unknown to me my eldest brother was passing through the same process, and had for some weeks kept away from the drink. All that week I was praying again and again for light, and did not find it. On the Thursday I was at a dancing, card-playing party until five in the morning, and it only increased my misery and despair.

I was glad when Sunday came, *my* Sunday! *My* emancipation day! The red-letter day of my life! *January 30th, 1876!* The tears of thankfulness are in my eyes, and a grateful joy is in my heart, as I think and write of it. Blessed day for me! and, thank God! blessed for multitudes more since then!

While preparing for chapel I heard my brother whisper to my sister that he intended to make a public decision for Christ that night. That was joyous hearing for me, for I had made up my mind to take the same step. On our way to the village I told my companion of my resolve, and was met with ridicule and the most sombre prophecies about my future. I needed no sermon, but we had one, for from the words "The Lord doth put a difference between the Egyptians and Israel" (Exodus xi. 7), Mr. Black preached with wonderful power. I needed no invitation to stay to the prayer-meeting, and that night my brother and I both gave ourselves to Christ and accepted and trusted Him as our personal Saviour. That night we both prayed among those earnest, rejoicing Methodists. That night, when we got home, we renewed our vows and determined never to be parted from the Lord to whom we had turned. From that day to this I have found His keeping power as wonderful as His saving grace.

CHAPTER III.

My Early Christian Life.

WHEN, on that blessed Sunday night, my conversion was announced in the village street outside the chapel, a man who knew me well, said: "Never, as long as there is a greyhound alive!" Excepting Mr. Black and two or three others, that man voiced the popular feeling in the district, and for the first seven days most of the Methodists even thought I was "having them on." But *I was tremendously converted*. When that became convincingly evident, the next cry was, "He will not stand!" They thought that the cards, the horses, the dogs, the drink, the dance, and the comic songs would soon drag me back. But I had got to a living Christ, who was equal to all my need, and such a thing as backsliding never entered my mind. All desire for my old haunts, companions, and sins left me at once, except my desire for strong drink. Not even my parents ever knew how intense that desire was. I was not then taught that Christ could there and then take that away; and, though never yielded to, the craving was with me for four years, and then it too entirely left me.

The sensation and talk in the neighbourhood were intensified when, a week after our conversion, my brother and I became members of the Wesleyan Society. I knew nothing of creeds or of polities, and no man ever joined a church in greater ignorance of its history, creed, and work. I am a Wesleyan to-day because of my profound conviction that in that communion I can serve God and my fellow-men better than in any other. But I had no such conviction then, and simply joined the band of Christians because through and among them I had become Christ's man. For that step I have been more than thankful ever since.

On my first saved Sunday I went to class, and then stayed to work in the Sunday-school, and felt there and then that I had to be a minister of the gospel. That first talk with a few boys resulted in one of them deciding for Christ, though he only told me of it years afterward when he himself was in the gospel ministry. In the presence of those earnest lads I became possessed of a desire to preach Christ to others, and at once began to read all that I could reach that might help me. I had made a clear break with the past during the week, having written to all my godless mates or seen and told them of my new experience and resolves. I had too broken off betting arrangements and burnt my cards, sporting papers and comic songs. Clear of past sinful entanglements, I began an earnest study of the Scriptures and any good books I could lay hands upon. At my conversion I possessed but one little religious book given me when a boy, but my little stock began to grow. How hungry I was for spiritual information! What distances I would walk to hear public men preach or lecture! How eager I was to get to every means of grace within my reach! What hours and hours I spent in conversation with Christians of longer experience than mine! How greedily I drank in truth, and how hard I tried to remember all I heard! I would walk any distance with a local preacher and sit or stand with him as long as he liked to talk of texts, sermons, and the word and work of God. I felt that precious years had been wasted, that I had a life-work to do, and that time had therefore become precious to me as never before.

A Temperance Society and Band of Hope had been formed, and I eagerly threw myself into that kind of work. Twelve weeks after my conversion I gave my maiden speech at a temperance meeting, and *intemperately* spoke for forty-five minutes. However the folks sat it out I cannot tell, but they did. Three weeks after that, in our own little chapel, when I was only fifteen weeks old in Christ myself, I preached my first sermon, from John iii. 14. Three weeks after that I preached my second sermon, and two weeks later I there preached my third sermon. It was on blind Bartimæus, and at the close I saw the first visible fruit of my ministry. That night a young farmer turned to God, who took charge of the class there when I left for the ministry, and who is a gifted local preacher to-day.

How I rejoiced over that seal to my preaching! How I thanked God with tears! I spent a lot of time in prayer in those days. When, after dinner, the rest of the men on the farm were resting, I was in some quiet corner with my Bible and praying for myself, for my dear ones and for all around me. Those sweet hours of prayer were an untold help to me, and I commend the practice to all young Christians who can follow it in these busy days.

Seeing my first convert strengthened my convictions about the ministry, and soon the Methodists around began to express theirs in the same direction. Before I was two years old in Christ I was looked upon as a "candidate for the ministry" and began to study specially with that in view. In these studies I was greatly helped by the Rev. James Duff, who had come to be our minister. I could only then speak in our broad Cumberland dialect, and he showed me how to cover less space with my vowels, and put me right about a host of pronunciations and provincialisms. I went once a fortnight to a Mutual Improvement class in Maryport, largely to learn how to speak English. Before we met at the chapel,

Mr. Duff used to examine me in the work—theological and scholastic—of the preceding fortnight, and mark me out a new lot. To his wise and kindly help I owe more to-day than I can ever express or repay.

As my father was not a Methodist, and could not possibly enter into the situation or understand my position, nearly all my study was extra work in spare hours. My every day was filled with the regular work, and I dared not ask for any time from that. I was jealous too of my religion and my Methodism, and determined not to do any less for my father because I had begun to work for Christ. The result was that nearly all my studies had to be done at nights, when the day's work was done, and often when all the rest of the family were in bed, or on the horses' backs going to and from the plough, and out on the roads with the carts. Apart from my devotional reading, I thus read the Bible twice through between being led to Christ and entering the ministry.

Not once but scores of times I have fallen asleep with my book in my hand, on the front of a cart, and fallen back into the cart, dropping my book in the road. I just stopped the horse, went back for my book, and again began to read. Dozens of times when sitting up alone until midnight or one or two in the morning, I have gone to sleep and fallen forward with my face on my book. Then I used to go into the out-kitchen, pump cold water from the well, splash my face with it, and then go back to my studies. For five months prior to my going to Didsbury College for the July examinations, for five nights per week, I only had three hours of sleep per night. It was during spring and summer, and every morning I had to rise at five and get the men out for their work. Except on Saturday and Sunday nights, just before and after my Sunday preaching, when I took a full night's rest, I used to study each night through until two in the morning.

No doubt it was a terrible tax on my constitution, but it had to be done if I were to enter the ministry. In those last two years I was acting overseer in our own parish, and road-surveyor for my uncle in the adjoining parish for one year and *vice versa* the other year, and kept my father's books, and managed the field department of the farm. At the same time I was class-leader, society steward, treasurer of the band of hope, and chairman of most of the temperance meetings at the chapel. I was also sick and death-bed visitor, and preaching nine or ten Sundays per quarter.

I got terribly in arrears with sleep, and when out with a cart at night in the dark I usually slept nearly all the way home. The mare I generally had in the cart could always find her way home safely through road or village, and I never had any mishap. The two or three policemen on those roads knew me well, knew what I was aiming at, and how hard I had to toil. When they met my mare and cart at night and did not see me, they knew I was asleep among the empty sacks; and the dear fellows never once gave me a wrong word. They would hit the side of the cart with a stick, and I would often wake up sufficiently to hear, "Now, Tom, that won't do, you know." I just mumbled "Good night" and went to sleep again. On keen frosty nights I often awoke by our yard gate frozen nearly stiff, but I never took any harm with it.

I had not a doubt about my call to the ministry, nor about my unfitness for it. I knew I must work hard if I meant to get in; and work hard I did, too. I knew I was strong in body, and never dreamt that I was in any way harming it; and because my heart was in it, the work was full of gladness.

In March 1879 the quarterly meeting recommended me as a candidate for the ministry, because they thought I had "grace," were sure I had seen "fruit," and felt that the ministry of the gospel was my sphere for the future. I preached my trial sermon previous to the synod, at Whitehaven. Before going to that service I had to administer corporal punishment to one who very much needed it. That upset me so much that I had a bad time in preaching, and I fancy the three ministers appointed to hear me had not a very good time. At any rate they did not give me a good mark for my sermon. But I had a fine time in the synod examination, and in spite of my sermon I was "sent on to the July committee."

I preached my next trial sermon in Carlisle, before the Rev. Henry Young, and had tea with him and his family before the service. The wise old saint told me not to mind my broad Cumberland speech, but think only of my message and hearers. He sat behind me, and not in front writing notes where I could see him. The result was that I *just forgot he was there* and that it was a trial sermon, and had a rare good time. I think he must have somewhat enjoyed it too, for he gave me a good mark and did his best for me later. I formed friendships in that service that are strong and precious with me to-day.

The first week in July came, and with sixty-three more candidates I found myself at Didsbury for the final examinations. More than one hundred and forty were offering themselves, less than a hundred were required, and during the week a lot of poor fellows were refused. The distress of two or three of them I remember still. Amid it all, I never had a doubt of the result. I felt sure of my call, and felt sure I had done all I could in the time to prepare myself.

So far as appearances went, I must have been the most unlikely candidate of the lot. In the fields all the day long, I was tanned as brown as a ripe nut. Standing over six feet high, in clothes of country cut, wearing a country style of red beard, and speaking a broader and more uncouth dialect than any one there,

I did not look or sound very clerical. When, on the last day, I had to pass the doctor he never put a hand on me, but just laughed and made the company laugh at the idea of my ailing anything. I remember, too, that in sheer irony he told the college governor who was present at the time, that if I came to Didsbury he must always have on hand a good supply of tonics in the shape of quinine and iron. But I was saved and had a great longing for the saving of others. The Lord, who had given me that desire to win souls, meant me to be where it could have its fullest expression. The examiners recognised that, and as I had a good time in the exams. I was accepted for "the Institution and Home Work."

I was filled with grateful joy on my acceptance, and yet with a solemn fear. I had very lofty ideas about the sacredness and responsibility of the Christian ministry, and, sure as I was about my call, and certain as I had felt about getting through, the tears were as close to the eyes as were the smiles to the lips. I am thankful that the old glad awe about my calling is with me still, that still I feel that to be a minister of the gospel of Christ is the most solemn as well as the gladdest calling in life.

The week that followed I shall never forget. After getting home and receiving the congratulations of my friends I almost collapsed. After the heavy strain of preparation and the excitement of Manchester and the exams. were over, the reaction came.

For the hard study after long hours on the farm, and especially for having had so little sleep for five months, Nature sent in her bill. I became almost listless and took little interest in anyone or anything. I could hardly sit down anywhere without falling asleep. On the Thursday I sat down in the kitchen of a friend at eleven in the morning and slept there till four in the afternoon. By the end of the week I had pulled together again, and was eager and ready to resume my studies on more advanced lines.

We were told that there would be no room in the colleges that year for any of the newly accepted candidates, and that we would be put on "the President's list," to be called into circuit work during the year, if wanted. I at once ordered Latin and Greek grammars and exercise books, and with a little valuable help from Mr. Duff I began the study of both languages. So it came about that my first knowledge of Greek and Latin was acquired on the roads, on the horses' backs or in the carts, or sitting up at nights when the rest of the household were in bed. I kept up those studies when, six months later, I was called to labour in a circuit. The result was that I was translating both languages when I went to college, and was very thankful for such elementary knowledge in these parts of my college work.

In February 1880 the young Wesleyan minister stationed at Airdrie near Glasgow resigned, and I was called from home to take his place as "supply."

That proved to be the only "circuit work" I ever had, and I am always thankful for the experiences it brought me. My superintendent was the Rev. Jabez Chambers, and a kinder and more considerate super. no young man ever had. He saw how terribly limited was my knowledge of Methodism and Methodist polity and usages, and his patience and helpful sympathy were those of a brother and friend. I had never been from home among strangers before; and he and his kindly wife soon made the manse at Coatbridge one of the happiest homes I ever entered.

On my first Sabbath evening at Airdrie there were just fifty-five people present, and I was told that it was a larger audience than usual, "to hear the new minister." There was only one class-meeting on the premises, and the weekly offertory had run down to less than nine shillings. This state of things I felt would never do, and I at once got to work. I looked up every person and family in the town that I could hear of ever having had any connection with Methodism. In this visitation work I was greatly helped by two or three earnest Durham miners, at that time living in Airdrie. I joined the strongest Temperance society in the town, and sometimes preached on the subject. Such work soon began to tell, and the audiences steadily increased. When people in ones and twos began to get converted, they increased still more rapidly till at the end of the six months the church was full of people and full of new life and hope.

In a village two miles away I engaged a Good Templars' room, spent two whole days in visiting, and started a Tuesday evening service. The Lord so blessed that work that when I left in the following August I had a class-meeting there with twenty-two members. Eight families were waiting to join our church in the town as members, if Conference would allow me to stay, and I wanted to stay. But it was not to be; those in authority said I must leave Airdrie and have three years in college, and they were wiser than I in the matter.

I had got to love the folks and the work so much that I felt it terribly when I had to leave them. My feelings then have ever since kept me in sympathy with most movements towards the stretching of the three years' system in our church. My people there were as simple as they were kind, and were as anxious for me to stay as I was myself. A few of them wanted to petition the President to make me an exception to the rule, but I was able to show them the futility of any such course, so they decided on a wiser one. During the six months of my ministry the weekly collections ran up finally to over fifty shillings. This cleared off arrears, and there was a balance of six pounds in the hands of the circuit steward. At a meeting held the night before I left the circuit they decided to give me those six pounds to pay my fare home, and in thanking them I heartily commended the wisdom of their decision.

In those six months I learned much of the life and work of the regular ministry, that has stood me in good stead. I saw, even in that narrow sphere, how much there is of serving tables, of putting thought and conscience into trivial things, of being patient and kindly and yet firm with childish members and queer officials, and of combating tendencies to worldly methods in spiritual work. In those six months I learned enough to make me sympathetic ever since with my brethren who are in regular circuit work, and to convince me that it is the backbone work of our church.

CHAPTER IV.

College Days.

IN September 1880 I was sent to Headingley College, Leeds, for three years of special training for my future ministry. Being twenty-seven years of age I was one of the oldest men who ever went, yet in Christian training and experience, and in knowledge of Methodism, I was one of the very youngest.

I went against the wishes of most of my Methodist friends in the North, who prophesied my ruin. Somehow the good folks up there had got the foolish notion that our colleges are institutions for taking from young men their evangelistic fervour and the keen edge of their own spiritual life. I believe in my heart that a greater mistake can hardly be made. My own experience was that if a man cannot live near to God and maintain a deep spiritual life in one of our colleges, he is not likely to do it anywhere. I was a better Christian, in closer personal fellowship with Christ, and of much more use to God and men, when I left college than when I went. Like every other life-sphere, college has its special perils, but it also has its special safeguards and helps. For nearly twenty-three years I have strenuously combated the notion that our colleges rob men of their spirituality and zeal, and teach them vanity and empty pride instead. College simply develops what is in the man to start with. If he be a donkey when he goes in, there is simply more and clearer ocular evidence of it when he comes out.

The late Rev. Benjamin Hellier was our governor, and with such a man at the head of the institution we were very highly favoured indeed. In matters of principle he was as firm as a rock, but he was also as gentle and kindly as a mother. His spiritual life was deep and mature, the welfare of the students was heavy upon his heart, and his dealings with us were as tender as they were manly and wise. There was no approach to anything like jealous espionage or surveillance. He just put us on our honour and trusted us, and of course that trust secured the fullest and most loyal kind of obedience. He was more a father than a governor to us, and we not only revered but also loved him; and out of our love we sought to please him. For instance; it was a college rule that no one was to smoke on the college premises or grounds. Several of the men loved a pipe and indulged in it when away on appointments or out among friends. Yet, I say it to the honour of the good fellows, I never once saw, smelt, or heard of tobacco smoke in that college, in all the three years of my residence.

Mr. Hellier's own preaching was not that of an evangelist, but that of a ripe and richly experienced Christian teacher; yet he was in deep and tender sympathy with all true evangelism, and so were all the tutors. In those days it was often assumed by decadent Methodists and superficial observers that evangelism was of necessity coarse and ignorant. Cold and lazy professors of religion used to sneer and assume that any man could be an evangelist who had not enough brains for any other style of preaching. Such flippant ignorance got no support either from our governor or the staff of tutors. We were taught that all ministerial work is one; that the work of the evangelist and that of the pastor and teacher are not contradictory but complementary. Whom God honoured our governor and tutors honoured, and our efforts to win men to Christ received their fullest and warmest encouragement. For my three years of study under the influence and teaching of such men, I am more thankful than any words of mine can tell.

And what a help it was, and what an education, to spend three years with such a set of students! Of necessity, they were nearly all the picked young preachers from our circuits, and nearly all splendid Christians and earnest preachers. They were happy helpful years that I would not have missed for a fortune. How the heart warms! How the tears rise! And again how the smiles follow the tears, as one thinks of those men and those days! There were men among them who in a special sense were looked upon as the "saints" of the college, others as the orators or evangelists of the years to come. Some were wise in the things of God and of life, and were sought unto as counsellors; and others, of sunny temperament and religious outlook, were the tonics resorted to in the time of cloud or depression: but nearly all were good men and true.

After stiff exams. and before holidays the gravest of us became merry. The tender pain of partings was soon forgotten in the thoughts of home and dear ones. The very reaction from the study and the sedentary life was with most of us but a lapse into innocent merriment or games. Puns we had galore, and of jokes and funny tales there was no end. Of sharp wit and keen satire there was no lack, but it was all given and taken in good humour and loving comradeship. At such times we were just *big boys*, and behaved as such.

But the other and deeper phases of life and feeling were there. We never forgot the future life-work, and the honest stern preparations for it were seldom shirked. However merry the moods, the hearts were right with God and men. If sorrow or difficulty came to one of us, he had the quick deep sympathy of all. If help was needed, it was gladly given without being asked. However boisterous the mirth, class and prayer meetings found few absent, and there a glad reverence was the atmosphere of the room. Aye, and there were inner circles of threes and fours who met for a more private communion of soul and intercession with God on behalf of those to whom we were sent to preach. How much some of us owe to those small prayer bands, only "the day will declare."

One of the amusing memories of those days is that of our unbounded conceit. Ministers of note, when dining at the college, were usually called upon to address us. When prominent ministers in our own or other churches came to Leeds to preach or lecture, we often went to hear them, and then reviewed and criticised their deliverances. And what criticisms they were! What a knowledge of history! What a profound scholarship! What a deep and wide knowledge of human nature and life! And what an amount of homiletical skill we put into those examinations! If those poor misguided preachers and lecturers had but known what men who knew all things thought of their efforts, they would have dared to face the public no more! There is no time in a man's life when he knows so much or is so competent to criticise others, as when he is at college. I realized that so clearly when I was myself one of the learned, that even now no audience makes me tremble or perspire so much as the students in one of our colleges.

And then there were our happy week-ends when out preaching. The change from college life to family life was to most of us as salutary in manners as it was sweet to the taste. Even in a college with sixty or more young men preparing for the Christian ministry, "it is not good for man to be alone." It is so easy to let bluntness become boorishness, to let free and easy greetings and intercourse drift into positive rudeness. But in the families of our people we came under the refining influence of female society, and found it a beautiful corrective of our rougher life during the week. Then too, the hours spent in those families reminded us of our own homes and dear ones, and so helped to keep their memories warm and tender in our hearts. Though only "students," our hosts and their families usually did all they could to make us happy and at home, and some of my dearest and happiest resting places in these days are in the homes in which I used to stay in those dear old college days. Friendships were then formed that are strong and tender to-day, and that have been an untold blessing to me from that time until now.

Perhaps I had fewer of those homes than most men at the college, but what I lost in numbers I expect I gained in depth and permanence. After receiving the great spiritual lift to be referred to later, my ministry became more than ever evangelistic. Nearly every Sunday night a number of penitent sinners turned to Christ in my service. Such work always appeals to true Methodists, and the result was that I went again and again to the same chapel and the same home. I preached on twenty-six Sundays of my college life in two circuits, and to several places I went five or six times in the three years. I liked that, and I like it still. The places I now delight most to visit are mostly those I have visited annually for the longest stretch of years.

Strong as I was, I found the sedentary life and indoor study a great tax after my life in the open air. As a set off I did a long walk nearly every afternoon except when out in my tract district or visiting the poor souls in the infirmary or workhouse. If fine, I usually walked out on Saturday to all appointments within ten or twelve miles, and back in the same way on the Monday morning. Some of the men wondered at this and called me "the walking prophet," but it did more than all else to keep me in health and fitness for my work. It was all needed too, for I was terribly ignorant of the laws of health in those days and did some very foolish things both in diet and work. During my first vacation I wrote in an essay competition during the day and conducted a mission at nights, and this after doing far more reading and study than was wise under such changed conditions of life. The result was that I suffered from periodical headaches that often interrupted my studies and that kept revisiting me for two or three years after I became a connexional evangelist.

The one event of my college life, standing out above all the rest, was a great spiritual crisis for which I shall ever be grateful to Almighty God. On commencing our work in September 1881, the men of my year had to translate the Acts of the Apostles from the Greek. Before we were through the second chapter my eyes were opened to my own need and God's promise to me of the fulness of the Holy Spirit. I had heard next to nothing of this when I first turned to Christ, but in the two succeeding Keswick Conventions I heard addresses on the subject by Rev. E. H. Hopkins and Rev. Webb-Peploe. Now the Holy Spirit began Himself to teach me on the matter. I saw very clearly that after Pentecost those early Christians had a fulness of Divine life and power to which I was a stranger. I realized that while I *had* the Spirit, I was not *filled with* the Spirit; that I had welcomed Him as *guest* but not yet as *host* in my heart. I also saw that this glorious fulness was as much for poor me as for Peter, James and John.

And then began the saddest month of my life, a month of pain and tears of which I am heartily ashamed this day; because a month of pain and tears springing entirely from my own folly and selfish fear of allowing God to have all His own way with me. As already intimated I was then out from college nearly every Sunday, by request. I expect that some well-meaning but misguided Methodists had told me that I would one day be a popular preacher, and I had been stupid enough to believe them and to have some desires after this thing. When brought face to face with my need of a personal pentecost and God's call to it, I followed my Lord "into the wilderness to be tempted."

The evil one whispered to me that if I ceased to make and preach my sermons on present lines, if I ceased to search and care for sweet bits, flowery language, and the things that please an audience, the people would cease to come and hear me. He told me that if I preached to *save* and not to *please* my hearers, if I went from what would *go best* to what would *save most*, my career as a popular preacher would be ended. I confess with shame that, for a time, I listened to his tempting nonsense.

He told me too that, if I got this fulness of the Holy Spirit, I should have to go to China as a missionary and that I would not like it. Two of my college friends,—Rev. W. H. Watson, still in China, and the late Rev. Joseph Bell,—had promised to go there. They and the late saintly David Hill were trying hard to get me to go too; and thus the devil fancied he saw another chance with me. I did not want to go; I loved my work in this country better. I know now that my Master never meant me to go, but He allowed the devil to use the test. Aye, and I had *to be willing to go* and to be willing *to preach in any style*, before I could have the spiritual baptism for which I was praying with tears every day

In New Testament plenitude the Holy Spirit could not come to the church until Christ had ascended. Until He was "glorified" the church could not have her pentecost; and what is true of the church is true of the individual Christian. With this wondrous power only the fully consecrated can be fully trusted. Fire is only safe with those who will rightly use it. Such Divine power is only entrusted to those who will use it for the Divine glory.

I realized in those sad days that the Holy Spirit is *fire*, that fire *burns*, and that burning is a painful process. I saw that some of my ambitions and desires would have to perish, and the parting with them seemed to be hard work. How childish and stupid it all looks now! I had not then learned what I know now, that a man is never completely his own until he is completely Christ's, that this fire only burns up that which we are better without, and that therefore the consecrated life is the blessed life.

In the early part of November I went to preach at Batley. After an address I gave in the Hick Lane Sabbath-school some twenty young men and young women made a public decision for Christ. At Cross Bank chapel at night similar results followed my sermon, and I was strangely excited and moved. I had never before witnessed such triumphs in my work. I went to my bedroom to think and pray and not to sleep. In a fashion that I could not misunderstand, I heard my Lord say to me:—"You have had a new experience to-day, such as you never had before. But it is only a promise of what I can and will do through you when you are fully useable in My hands. Let self die, and put Me in the heart and front of your preaching, life-sphere and everything. Then the fulness for which you plead will be given to you, and what you have seen to-day you will find to be but a prophecy of greater blessings to come." Thank God for that day! Thank God for the next night at college!

I wanted no supper that Monday night, and left the dining room immediately after prayers. When I got into my study I locked the door, put my Bible open at Acts ii. on the chair, and fell on my knees in an agony of prayer and tears. I could hold out no longer. My whole being looked up to God and said, "None of self and all of Thee!" I remember saying; "I will go to China or anywhere else at Thy call, dear Lord, and preach in any style Thou choosest, only give me that for which I cry. I want what these early Christians got at pentecost. It is my birthright in Jesus, and for me as for them. I need it as much as they did; and perishing men and women in Yorkshire, and wherever I may go, need me to have this, as Jerusalem and Samaria needed these men and women to have it. I am willing, Lord, and I claim and trust. I can do no more, the rest is Thine." And, bless His name! He did it too!

I shall never forget that hour. There was no joyous exaltation or deep inrush of emotion, but a great calm. The quarrel was ended; my controversy with my Lord was over, and my soul was full of a great glad peace. I just took the Lord at His word. Knowing I had done my part, I was sure He must have done His; and I left the future and its results with Him. I decided to walk by faith and not by feeling in the matter, as I had urged penitent sinners to do when they were seeking pardon. I determined that if I did not see any more wonderful results I would keep on believing and assuming that I was "filled with the Holy Ghost." My faith was justified. For two or three weeks there was no apparent difference in the results of my preaching. But I kept on trusting, and then the "signs and wonders" of my longings, hopes and prayers began to come. At Radcliffe-on-Trent on the first Sunday in December the whole church was stirred, and a string of fine young men and women turned to God. In Nottingham, on one Sunday in the following January, seventy people sought the Lord in the sabbath-school and in the chapel. Wherever I went, kindred results attended the word, and my soul was a song of thankfulness to God. I give to Him all the glory and praise when I say that from my claiming my personal pentecost to my leaving college some twenty months later, I saw eighteen hundred souls led to Christ in my meetings, and that since then those numbers have reached nearly ninety thousand men, women and children. The more I think of it the more I am humbled before

God, and the more every fibre of my being feels and says: "Not by might, nor by power, but by My Spirit, saith the Lord of Hosts."

CHAPTER V.

Connexional Evangelist.

THE personal pentecost described in our last chapter made me *an evangelist*. No doubt the calling was there, the desire, and some qualifications of temperament and physique, but needing this baptism of fire to make them effective. Until then, though nearly always on Sunday evenings I preached for definite decisions for Christ, and again and again saw such results, the preaching I loved best was that of the Christian teacher; even now, my preparation for and preaching to Christians are my great delight. But since then the greatest part of my life-work has been calling sinners to repentance.

My experience was no isolated one. Moody told us that he preached for years without seeing many conversions. Then he sought and claimed the fulness of the Spirit, and at once saw "signs and wonders" under his ministry. The very sermons that had previously been almost barren, in producing results, became the means of leading multitudes of

Mr. Waugh's Father and Mother.

people to Christ. Henry Drummond came into contact with Moody and his work, was filled with the holy flame, and became God's evangelist to the cultured and scholarly sons of Scotland and other lands. The gifted pastor of Highbury Quadrant church was for long years the Christian teacher and author, chary of evangelists and evangelism. He saw his need of and received a personal pentecost, and in amazement, two continents recognize and welcome him as a fervid evangelist and winner of souls. One might mention a string of men toiling with mighty success among us now, who a few years ago knew little or nothing of passion for souls. But they were put into positions of great responsibility which threw them back hard upon God. There He got full possession of them and they of Him, and in His passion and power they became mighty to turn men to the Saviour. I am, and have for a long time been, persuaded that if the Christian church were to claim that fulness of the Holy Spirit which is her birthright, her equipment, the greatest of all her needs, the proportion of what we call evangelists, to pastors and teachers, would be very much larger than it is at present. Touched with this flame, not only a multitude of ministers, but of the laity, who have hardly tasted the ecstasy of soul-winning, would joyously respond to God's call with a fervent "Here am I, send me!" Aye, and then He could and would send them, and they would come back laden with trophies of victory.

Before that time I had loved my Lord and tried to serve Him, but never as since then. Before that anointing I had tried, with many failures, to give Him joy, but that longing then became a passion. I saw too that the greatest joy I could give Him through service was the joy which is His compensation for "the travail of His soul,"—the joy of receiving and saving His blood-bought ones.

"The fruit of the Spirit is love," of men as well as of God, and I was led into a tender love of my fellow-men and a deep sympathy with their lost estate, such as I had in the past been a stranger to. My own relations to my Lord were so much closer and happier that I became possessed of a passionate yearning that others should know my Saviour and have the bliss that had come to me. This love and longing made itself felt in my congregations; and, God working through it, the people were led to Christ and saved.

Alexander M'Aulay, Thomas Champness, and a few other wise and saintly men who were keen evangelists, saw what had come to me and what the work was for which the Master had been fitting me. They were convinced that my work was to be that of the evangelist, and the Conference of 1883 endorsed their convictions. My last year at college was Thomas Cook's first year as a connexional evangelist. Of the wonderful work the Lord accomplished through him in the years just preceding that time, and for long years after, there is no need to write here. The story is well known, and its fruits are world-wide to-day. Thus it came about that I left college to join him, and we were colleagues for a period of twenty years. In the earlier years of our comradeship we worked a great deal together and I owe more through God's blessing to that time of fellowship, in thought, prayer and service than I can possibly put into words.

I am in my twenty-third year in this work, have travelled over 250,000 miles, and averaged 350 services per year. My health has been such that, though I have sometimes missed a service or two, I have not missed a *mission* for more than twenty-one years. I have never once doubted my call for such work, and I love it more now than ever before, though it is now much more difficult than at the beginning. When Mr. Cook and I were appointed, we had the field almost to ourselves and almost wherever we went it was "white unto harvest." Such missions were comparatively new, except where Moody and Sankey had been, and the people flocked to them in crowds. In relation to such work they generally found virgin soil too, and were susceptible to the distinctly evangelistic appeal. They had not then become adepts at refusing such offers of life, and often a twelve days' mission resulted in eight or nine hundred and sometimes more than a thousand inquirers.

It is different in these days ; the work is very much more difficult, and in most cases the visible results are not so many. To the power and results of such work as Moody's, Hay Aitken's, and ours, was added the intensely urgent and aggressive note of the Salvation Army. The churches all round were stirred up to a holy emulation, especially in regard to their duties to the masses at the bottom of society. In addition to evangelists working in direct connection with the churches, a whole host of free-lance evangelists, male and female, came into the field, often with disastrous results. Mission chapels, halls, and rooms sprang into existence in all the large towns and cities, and became centres of revival appeal. Earnest Christians *would have* missioners ; and if accredited ones were not to be had, people full of zeal but devoid of judgment, would have anybody who could shout in prayer and say " Come to Jesus."

By the crude and repellent theology of many of the latter class, and by their oft-time questionable methods in seeking to secure visible results at any price, evangelism has often been hard hit, and grave injury has been inflicted on a noble and necessary work. Then too there is now quite a little army of us Wesleyan evangelists, ministerial and lay, working under our own Home Mission Committee ; a similar company, headed by Gipsy Smith, work in connection with the Free Church Council ; an army of " Joyful News " lads and deaconesses are constantly missioning in the villages; the big centres are visited by such stalwarts as John McNeill and George Clarke; and most of the people in the poorer city neighbourhoods have been evangelised by the Salvation Army. The novelty and freshness are now gone from missions and their methods. Instead of being "special" they have become the order of the day. In scores of churches the regular work is foolishly discredited and the people missioned to death. Some earnest but mistaken people fancy they are disloyal to God and the people, and losing grace themselves, unless they have a mission every year.

The time-spirit too has become more than ever against spiritual work, except during the last twelve months, when the Welsh revival has sent a saving throb through the land. The present-day passion for personal pleasure, the craze for excitement of a physical sort, makes people less inclined to things spiritual and more impatient of their restraints. The world's call to temporal pleasure is so tempting and insistent, that voices calling men to the eternal realities often fall on unheeding ears. Then again there is less initial faith, less of the disposition to take the gospel and its claims for granted, than there used to be. Some results of the Higher Criticism have helped all who understand them; but a lot of the assertions of the Higher Conceit, and antagonism to a Divine revelation, have done a great deal of sad unsettling work among those who do not understand, but who are only too ready to welcome any apparent loosening of the Divine sanctions. That they may be able to drink, bet and sport, and become mere animals, with an easier conscience, thousands of men have swallowed the dogmatic negations and baseless assertions of "Nunquam." While such thinkers as Huxley, Tyndall, Herbert Spencer, and other men with brains have looked behind things seen and said "I do not know," this latter-day prophet of those who do not think sets out to demonstrate a negative; and he and they try to imagine that he has succeeded.

But if these things make the work of the evangelist more difficult, and limit the amount of raw material within his reach, the work is none the less needed and none the less owned of God. And, if the work is not on so large a scale, one has all the better opportunity of making it deeper, both during the mission and in the nursing and educational stages that follow. Some of the reasons why my zest for this work and enjoyment of it are just as keen as twenty years ago, I will now state in order to help younger evangelists who may read these pages.

As soon as I left college and entered this special work some of its perils became very apparent to me. I saw for instance that it offered a strong inducement to intellectual laziness if a man had a tendency that way, and had not a tender conscience about hard work. Once he has got a score of evangelistic appeals, and a few addresses on holiness and Christian work, a man may for a number of years go on as a missioner, without any strong consecutive reading and thinking. He may give the same addresses for long years as he moves from place to place, and still do some good saving work.

But, though easy, that is a fatal course, and in time must terribly limit a man's outlook and grip, and kill his mental fertility. The Holy Spirit had not said His last word to men when the canon of the New Testament was completed. He is still speaking through widely different people and in wonderfully different ways. This is so true that I believe that no preacher can neglect deep and wide reading without stultifying his mental powers and narrowing his possibilities of usefulness.

I am very thankful that I saw this danger when I entered this work, and determined to keep up my habits of reading and study. To help me in this I have tried to keep in touch with all the great questions and problems filling the best hearts in the Christian church, in social life, and in the nation. I have done a course of reading and study on the subjects of these great movements of thought and feeling, and have then given the results of my observations and studies in the form of public lectures. Perhaps my readers will understand and pardon my motive if, for the sake of the young preachers I am specially writing to help, I mention a few of these subjects of my reading and lecturing. In some of these subjects, such as socialism, current science, the inspiration of the Bible, nonconformity, and sacerdotalism, I did an earnest course of reading for two years or more before I ventured to discuss them in public. Among the subjects of my lectures have been, "Is life worth living?" "Is Christianity played out?" "Christ and the present life"; "Why I am a Nonconformist"; "England's danger:—the priest"; "The Millennium"; "The national outlook from a Christian standpoint"; "Two national perils, and how to meet them"; "The 'Clarion' or the Bible"; "Has man a free will?" "Is the Bible un-scientific?" and, "Is the Gospel a failure?"

I have always felt that we ministers, who are set apart by the church and freed from all pressure of business and care about the daily bread, owe it to the people who are not thus set free, to be readers and students. We owe it to them to use our time in the fields they have not time to traverse, and to give to them the results of our honest toil. And what a personal gain it is too! The reading on subjects like these, in a sense outside one's evangel, keeps fresh currents of thought flowing through one's mind, keeps one in touch with the problems that perplex our hearers in their daily battle with the world, and so helps us to come back to the evangelistic appeal with renewed personal freshness of thought and feeling, and with a wider clearer knowledge of its application and the need for its message.

Closely akin to the help I have got from reading and thinking for my lectures is that I have received from giving pastoral preaching a large place in my ministry. When in "off weeks" between missions and during the summer months I am out lecturing, I always preach specially to help Christians in my afternoon services, as on all Sunday mornings. This not only keeps one's ministry from becoming one-sided, but the study of the word of God, and the reading preparatory to such preaching, are a great personal help and blessing. In preparing evangelistic addresses one is dealing always with the elementary truths of the gospel, and in such preaching everything has to be made to lead to a definite and immediate decision for Christ. Though building upon them, these foundation truths have been left behind in our own Christian experience; and in preparing and delivering sermons on them there is not much of help for our own spiritual life. But in ministering to other Christians, and in gathering the wherewith to minister to them, our own souls are fed and watered of God. My keenest joy is in such preaching; and hundreds of testimonies tell me that such messages will live and bless the hearers when the mission addresses to the unsaved have been forgotten.

Then again, this will be the ninth book I have written, and writing for others compels me to read for myself and for them. By publishing sermons and addresses one makes further use of them in the pulpit impossible; and this again strengthens the need for and incites to constant study and reading for new messages. My long and careful study of the Scriptures before writing "When Jesus Comes" was an unspeakable blessing to me, and led me into a study of eschatology in the Scriptures and in the history of dogma, which becomes more interesting and delightful as the years pass. I am grateful to God this day for the blessing He has seen fit to put upon my pen. Many souls, especially young men, have been led to Christ through "The Power of Pentecost" and "The 'Clarion' or the Bible"; and, through them all, multitudes of the people of God have been helped and blessed. Scores, of or from whom we have heard, have found peace with God while reading my booklet, "Words of Counsel to Young Christians," which has reached a circulation of 450,000.

Some six years ago the Methodists at Brampton asked me to help them to build a new chapel and Sunday-school. For a small cause in a country town, and with practically no wealthy members, the scheme was an ambitious one, and I promised to help. Since then I have had the joy of handing over to the trustees nearly nine hundred pounds, being the gifts of friends and profits from my books. I am glad to place on record the fact that, since promising to help this scheme with my book profits, the sale of them has been doubled. Apart from the booklet, some 85,000 of my books have been sold in this country alone. The late Mr. Moody took a fancy to my "Power of Pentecost" and published it in America. I asked for no royalty, knowing how he used such profits; but he sent me ten pounds for the Brampton chapel as a thank-offering for the blessing God had made the book in America. The last I heard from there about it was of a circulation of nearly a quarter of a million.

Another enjoyable feature of our work is our system of revisiting past mission spheres and preaching at our popular watering-places in the summer when we are not in mission. To go back to scenes of spiritual victories "to see how they do" is apostolic, and is a very happy and helpful experience both for the missioner and for the people on the spot. It deepens gratitude to God and strengthens faith, to be thus reminded of past triumphs of the gospel. It gives the converts something to look forward to, that under God may help them to stand fast and to work hard for their new Master. It may sound very human, but there is often a close and tender bond between the missioner and his children in the gospel. Happy friendships are then renewed, and the impulse to pray for each other is refreshed and quickened. I look upon my re-visits as among the happiest and most helpful of my experiences, and the same is true of my seaside week-ends where I meet with troops of friends and converts, and often reach, and help to Jesus, people we could not reach under any other conditions.

In these twenty-three years I have laboured in nearly every part of England and Wales, in Edinburgh, Glasgow, Dublin, Belfast, Cork, the Channel Islands and in the Isle of Man. In every place I have had a good home among kind people who were in full sympathy with my work. Many of those homes of past years are choice and happy resting places in these days, and their kind and godly inmates lie near and warm to my heart. In nearly every case too the ministers have earnestly sympathised with and helped us, and all the spiritually-minded members in the churches have done their best to help the work to a victorious issue.

Methodism was born in a distinct revival, and her history is largely a history of revivals. The saving of men is at once her mission and her genius, and this is most completely her passion when she is nearest to God and most loyal to the work He has called her to accomplish. One result is that earnest common-sense evangelism appeals to and wins the hearts of all true Methodists, aye and of all evangelical Christians in all the churches. I never felt this so forcefully as since my wife and I so tragically lost our firstborn in the awful railway disaster at Hall Road last July. The display of love and kindness given by the Christians of Southport bound us to the place by ties that we never dreamt were possible. On the day after our precious laddie left us, nearly two hundred telegrams came in, and on the Saturday over five hundred letters full of loving sympathy and comfort. Still they poured in from all parts of Britain, and a little later, from America, Canada, Africa, India, China, the Bahamas, the Continent and from Sweden, till nearly seventeen hundred such assurances came as expressions of the loving sympathy of God.

The writers represented nearly all creeds and churches, and represented congregations standing up and often weeping, all the land over. From the President of our Conference, the Bishop of Liverpool, the President of the Free Church Council, from nearly two hundred Wesleyan ministers, and from scores of pastors of other churches, came those messages of Christian love. They came to be read with thankfulness, though through tears, from our Conference, then sitting, from Keswick Convention, from services in churches, chapels, halls, Railway Missions and little gatherings of Brethren and Friends. They all told the same tale of sympathising love, and gave the same assurances of continued prayer. They came, God-sent, to my broken-hearted wife and me; but we knew they came largely through a love born of the saving work God had enabled us to do for Him.

And I want to say here, with all my heart in my words, that a great part of my life-work would have been an absolute impossibility but for the loving self-sacrifice and prayerful sympathy of the wife God has given to me. She was led to Christ before I knew her, in my first mission in Barnsley, and a deep sympathy with such work has ever since possessed her heart. She has given me up to the work, and borne the burden of the home and the training of our children ungrudgingly, though sometimes in heart-ache and tears. When the work has been trying and my faith sorely tested, the cheer of her messages and the knowledge of her prayers have been a source of real strength and help to me.

Of all the results of my work, nothing fills me with such grateful joy as the way God has used me in the saving of *my relatives.* The joy of all personal joys to me is the fact that up to now thirty-two of my own dear ones have been led to Christ under my own ministry. Though it was, of course, unseen by us at the time, the conversion of my wife has meant more to me than all the rest. The sweetest of all these to my own soul and to my wife's was when in my last mission in Barnsley our departed laddie, then a boy of ten, and our precious lassie still with us, and then but eight years old, entered the inquiry room as a public avowal of their love for Jesus. No words of mine can tell, but my readers can guess, how such blessings from God have made sacrifice easier, and toil lighter, and have helped to make and keep me grateful for my opportunities as a connexional evangelist.

CHAPTER VI.

Methods (Personal).

I AM being constantly asked to advise younger evangelists in such matters as habits of thought, work, and prayer in preparation for mission services; and I am often asked to give them a sketch of my own course in these things. Much of this is largely between one's self and God, and therefore a delicate matter and not for the public eye or ear. Still, though in many of these matters no man can be a law unto another, there are a few of my personal methods, which stated here may be made a blessing of God to others.

To begin with, I am certain that the first and most important preparation for Christian work of any kind is the *preparation of the worker.* The five outlets for the Divine life within us are the *character*, what we are ourselves; the *lips*, what we *say* to others; our *service*, what we *do* for others; our *money*, what we *give* to others; and our *prayers*, what we ask for and *claim* for others. The first of these, though not so far-reaching as the last, is the most important of them all. What we *are* largely determines the character and effectiveness of what we *say*, *do*, *give* and *pray*. It is *the life* behind them that determines the power of our words, our work, our gifts, and our intercession for others. It is with the first of these connections that we are now concerned, the relationship between the messenger and his message.

If the life be right the message will be in power. The grammar may be faulty, the pronunciation broken and faltering, and the words not the most suitable; but if the speaker be right *with God*, and therefore right *before men*, his speech will tell for both. We have all heard such men, and our hearts have burned as we listened to them. We forgot the halting sentences and inelegant words and figures, in the Divine grip and burn of them. The personality of the man reached us with his message, and through the Spirit of God touched and blessed us. Aye, and we have all heard a man claim to speak for God, who was no Divine messenger and who had no message. He may have been eloquent and scholarly, and his words beautiful and well placed, but powerless to bless. There was no spiritual glow or bite about them, and they slipped off the hearers as smoothly as they slipped out of the speaker.

It is the life that tells, and a deep full personal spiritual life is the first fitness for proclaiming the

Word of Life. We are spiritual as we are God-possessed, and spirituality is the very soul of use-ability. I was led to see this at the beginning of my ministry, and hence my first care has ever been with my own relations to God and fitness for being used of Him in my work.

In my last conversation with the late Rev. C. H. Spurgeon I asked him about his habits of quiet and prayer just before his preaching. His reply was:— "I try to live in the spirit of prayer all the day long, brother Waugh. The result is that, when the time for a service approaches, I have not to work myself up into a spirit of fitness for it, but I am living in that spirit all the time. I just come into this study and remind the Lord that I am going to preach, that it is His business and not mine, that He has promised to help me and make the word a blessing, and that I expect Him to keep His word. Then I go to the Tabernacle expecting a blessing, and I am not disappointed." It was beautiful and inspiring to see the dear man as he said this, and I was grateful for such a privilege. But, while Mr. Spurgeon was a great and good man, his method is not mine.

Of course, I try to live in the spirit of prayer and fitness for my work in the pulpit, all the day long. But *I must have* a time of perfect quiet with God, half an hour at the least, if possible, before I go to preach the gospel to the unsaved. My thoughts and feelings have for most of the day been centred in letters, reading, thinking, friends, and the circle of life around me. Now, alone with God, I want them called in, settled and calmed or stirred in prayer, occupied with God, with His message, and with those to whom I am to deliver it. I must have that time with God if I am to have a good time with men. If in the church I am to have the atmosphere in which the Holy Spirit does His grandest work, to have access to the holiest in public prayer, and to have a saving grip over my hearers in preaching, I must first win the victory alone with God.

I can think of a few times in my past ministry when there was no time for such prayerful seclusion; and there was no victory following. However innocent the cause of my missing my half-hour, however earnest and godly the people who helped me to miss it, I had not the atmosphere one carries direct from one's knees to the pulpit. I went to the pulpit without the world-excluded communion with God in which one's consciousness of ambassadorship, one's vision of God, one's faith in God and the spiritual realities, one's sympathy with the audience to be faced, and one's burdening with a message for them, are all renewed and strengthened. Consequently I was not the quick responsive channel between God and my audience that I should have been, and to that extent I was shorn of my power to reach and bless them.

Akin to this is my habit of having all my forenoons to myself when in mission and not travelling.

My rule for years has been to see no one from breakfast and family prayers until called to dinner. After further private prayer and devotional reading of the word of God, I read a portion of some helpful devotional book that I am careful to take with me. After that and the writing of letters, I give the time to reading and study, general and for sermons and lectures. These forenoons I claim most rigidly, and it takes a great deal to make me relax my rule. To the opportunities they give me I owe a great deal in my work for which I am very thankful.

And then again I have from the beginning had my longer periods for secret communion with God and with His holy word. I am no recluse or hermit, but, I think, pretty full and fond of social life and feeling. I enjoy the company of good people and their times of innocent merriment. After the spiritual strain of a service or meeting, at the supper table or later by the fireside, I am happy in the pleasantries of Christian social fellowship. For my being able to leave the service in the church, and to share in the stories, reminiscences and laughs at the fireside, I stand my work all the better, and feel sure I shall live all the longer.

But the more I am in company the more I must be alone; the more I am with men the more I must be with God: the more I am among and before the crowd the more I need to be where I can hear God speak to me. The rush of life is so swift in these days, its duties so many, and its calls and claims so urgent, that the hungry soul must be imperative about its times in the secret place with God. Social duties and church organisations are so multiplied that too few Christian toilers get "into the mount" for more than a few minutes at a time. Those who do have almost to make the time and hold to it through all things.

My earliest readings of the Scriptures showed me the place and value of such times of retirement with God for the prophets of God. Before he led a host of people from Egypt, Moses was in the lone place seeing the burning bush and hearing the voice of God. From the ravine of the lonely Cherith and the quiet upper chamber at Zarephath, Elijah came to Carmel to defeat the priests of Baal and strike Divine conviction to the heart of a nation. Our Lord was thirty years in preparation for His wonderful ministry before He entered upon it. It was from the wilderness that the rugged Baptist came to shake the heart of Israel and proclaim the advent of the kingdom of heaven. Paul had his long quiet time in Arabia before he began his marvellous ministry for his Lord. Some of Luther's greatest triumphs followed his times of seclusion and preparation. Bunyan's immortal picture of the pilgrim life was born in his Bedford prison cell. It has ever been so, and my times of quiet at home, at Christmastide and Easter, and in the woods and fields round Brampton in the summer, have been my saving pauses in the racket and strain of my life. There my covenant with God was renewed; there the fellowship between the Master and the messenger entered into renewed freshness and reality; and there in the presence of God was born a deeper sympathy for perishing men. There the weary powers were rested and the spent forces restored; and there my Lord, His purposes, my own salvation and my mission, became again so real and vivid to me that all temptation to be mechanical and perfunctory was scattered, and from there I came back to my work to win victories for God among men.

Another habit that has grown upon me as the years have passed is that of *a constant and absolute reliance upon the Holy Spirit* for success. The more the Lord has chosen to use me, the more I have been humbled before Him. The greater the victories in which I have shared, the more my heart has said, "What am I and what my father's house?" The more sinners are saved and saints strengthened and helped under my ministry, the more I feel my own impotence, and that the blessing is of the power Divine. When I have done my very best in reading, in thinking, in keeping my body in the best possible working order, and in my preparation of myself and my message, I have no hope of victory except as I lean and get the people of God to lean upon the power of the Holy Ghost.

This is *the* secret of any success that has been given to my ministry. I am thankful to God that the thing most fully realised during and spoken of after my missions is the deep glad sense of the presence of God.

I look to Him myself as the source and guide of the mission. I urge the members of the church to join me in looking to Him for His guidance in our choice of methods, of hymns, and of message, day after day. Honouring Him we are honoured of Him, and we triumph through His manifested power. I seek to be kept free from thought, word, or deed that could grieve Him and in any way hinder His using me to the full, and always seek in the beginning of a mission to lead all my workers to the same spirit of absolute self-surrender. I point out that an unforgiving and other un-christian spirits, unhealed quarrels, uncharitable backbiting and tale-bearing, dishonesty and impurity in any form, and all kindred expressions of the flesh, are limitations of the power of the Holy Spirit and consequently hindrances to His full gracious working in our midst. I remind them that I am only one more toiler among them for a few days, that I am but a man needing the Divine power and guidance as they do, and urge them to look away beyond and behind me, and base all their faith and hopes upon the power of the Spirit of God. I point out that the work is neither mine nor theirs, and we cannot do it; that we are only the channels through which He works and thus makes us successful "co-workers together with Him." Thus, with the missioner and the church fully given up and looking up to Him, the Holy Spirit gets His way and that way is the way of victory.

And now in reference to personal habits in relation to saving work, I come to a delicate theme, in which I must walk carefully, and that is *the care and use of the body.* Though, as already intimated, I sprained some of the muscles of my heart by doing a man's heaviest work when I was but a thin growing lad, I was not aware of it at the time, nor for long years afterwards. In that ignorance, I slaved at college and in the first eleven years of my connexional evangelism, as if I was made of iron. The work is hard and trying enough even when one is most careful, but in those years I did a great deal of unnecessary work and foolish things, that made the strain still greater. Of course I did it without a dream of its inflicting lasting injury upon my body; but I was responsible for my ignorance, and have had to pay the price.

At its easiest, work like mine must of necessity be a heavy strain. For eight months each year it is one long soul-wrestle with the evil one and his world-forces, for the souls of men. It means therefore a constant watchfulness and burden for souls, and a constant heartfelt intercession for them. After such soul-strain one cannot preach to the perishing without the whole being going out to them in hunger for their decision for Christ. It is sometimes such a travail as only the evangelist can understand, and it is this passion of longing that makes a mission address take so much more life out of a preacher than a pastoral sermon to the people of God.

Then think of *the physical conditions* under which we usually work. I tell the folks on the first day of a mission that there are three things essential to a successful service;—*Divine power, gumption,* and *oxygen.* I point out that while the Lord provides the first, and the preacher the second, the caretaker and the chapel stewards are responsible for the third. But even then it is often very hard work to get some decent ventilation and some fresh air. I know of no one who needs more God-given grace and patience than a chapel-keeper. I pity such men with all my heart. They have a lot of people to please, some of them very queer people, and many of these people are the opposites of each other in their views and fancies about ventilation. Some find it too hot just while others are shivering, and some are clamouring for more ventilation while others are complaining of too much. Poor chapel-keepers! Aye, and poor evangelists! We get a lot of *soakings* and *suffocatings* that we would be glad to miss.

Thousands of times our places have been packed in every nook and corner, and hundreds of times hundreds of people have had to be turned away. There is nothing that brings people to God's house like other people being converted. When Lazarus gets raised, the people flock to Bethany to see him. Soon as the breakdown comes in the mission, the crowds come to see and share in it. Then, when the chapel is too small, they come early, and hundreds of times I have had to start before the time, in some cases more than a full hour before. All this means that the fresh air in the place is largely exhausted before the evangelist begins his work. He starts the service in a vitiated atmosphere, and breathes in a mischievous lot of carbonic oxide and animal matter instead of oxygen. It is worst of all in manufacturing towns where most of the people work in mills where the temperature is kept very high. The dear souls are like salamanders, they dread the sight of an open window, and almost sneeze at the mention of fresh air. All this is terribly trying to the system, and terribly lowers the vital tone. I have often been in such poison-shops from two to four hours at a stretch, and paid part of the price in pain when I have got to my home. And scores of times I have had to go to a fire and put on dry under-clothing before I dare sit down to supper.

To these harmful conditions I for years added many sad mistakes. Instead of resting in the summer, I put into it a lot of swimming, rowing, and mountaineering, which all meant additional strain upon the heart. In the same direction was my preaching in the open air to large crowds on Sunday afternoons, on the sands at Rhyl, Bridlington, and

Morecambe, and on Douglas Head, when I ought to have been laid on my back. I am still an enthusiastic believer in open-air preaching, and I believe that the very best preaching a man can do is necessary there of all places; but *it should not be put in between two crowded services* inside a church, in addition to an after-meeting and work in the inquiry room.

In those early years I too often forgot that "the sabbath was made for man," and very often went without one, filling up every night with a mission service. Now, I insist on having my sabbath rest, only my work compels me to be a Jew and take my sabbath on Saturday. Then too I used to take an afternoon service three or four days a week. Now I find it better in a mission to take only one such service per week, and take a walk and some fresh air on the other afternoons. I have on some occasions given as many as three open-air addresses in one evening. While urging all the Lord's toilers to work up to the last ounce, and put all in that is possible "while it is day," it is a sad mistake to shorten the "day" unnecessarily and hasten "the night . . . when no man can work."

Our bodies are a sacred trust and to be treated as such. They are the casket of the soul, the life, and it is through the powers of the body that the life within finds expression. Our bodies are the machinery through which the indwelling Spirit of God works out His glorious purposes by us. And they are also temples indwelt by God, and to be so kept for Him, that He may get the most possible out of them for His glory and the blessing of those around us. We are to see therefore that we neither eat nor drink nor work to the injury of the body and its unfitting for such indwelling and using of God. I am not playing the teacher in saying these things, but out of my own mistakes and their consequences I am offering a word of kind but solemn warning to the eager and enthusiastic young Christians who may read these lines.

And one word more. I know that I started life with a strong constitution; I know that tens of thousands pray for me and my work and that the answers to their prayers help me even in my body; yet I am certain that I could not possibly have come through these twenty-two years without missing a mission, had I not been *sparing in my diet.*

I have felt sure for years that most people eat too much, especially of animal food. I am sure too that the more sedentary, intellectual and nervous our work, the less animal food we ought to take. For years I have taken no meat, bacon or eggs in the morning, or at tea, only something light to keep off hunger. This means animal food twice a day, and often I do not take it more than once. Even then I never under any conditions take *a heavy meal.* I am better in health in every way for light meals, and for living mostly on stewed fruits and vegetables instead of meat. Through having only a few pieces of dry toast and a cup of tea to breakfast, I can read, write, and study twice as well in the forenoon; and through having a similar tea in the afternoon I can preach with greater ease at night.

I offer no theories to others and recommend no nostrums, but I have learned that when I have little in my stomach I have more blood and nerve force free to help my brain. I have learned that it is not what we eat, but what we are able to assimilate, that is of any use to us, and that all food beyond that is but a tax and strain on the system. I have learned therefore that I am lighter, clearer, brighter, happier, and more active in body, mind and nerve, as I eat and drink sparingly in view of my work, and not at all between meals, or heavily at meals, to gratify my appetite. This course has been so great a blessing to me that I fearlessly mention it to those who are toilers for God, but not engaged in manual labour, where more animal food may be needed.

Chapter VII.

Methods (Public).

HERE again in many ways every toiler must be a law unto himself. We differ so widely in temperament and in mental outlook that the methods adopted by one soul-winner, however successful, may be quite impossible to another. Nevertheless, as my handbook on "Special Missions" ran through 5,000 copies in eighteen months, and has been out of print for four years, and as I am still constantly written to for advice as to public methods in conducting missions, I venture in this volume one chapter on the subject.

On *the human side* the most important thing of all, in the work of saving men, is persistent, believing, claiming *prayer*. The Old and New Testaments alike teach that *persistency* is one of the most important features of all successful praying for the souls of men. In all such prayers, as Mr. Gordon so clearly points out, there are three persons concerned: *the man* who prays; God, *to Whom* he prays; and Satan, *against whom* he prays. In His temptation, His ministry, His passion, His death, and in His resurrection, the rightful Prince, Jesus, has defeated and routed the usurping prince, Satan. But He has left him in the field of battle, and the campaign is not ended, though the greatest victory has been won.

By *this right* of conquest men now belong to Christ, but He will only take them by *their own consent.* He will not wrest them *by force* from the enemy who holds them, but seeks to win them *by love.* Saved men and women are the allies of Jesus in this conflict, and a wonderful honour it is to us! I hear good people say in sermon, song, and prayer that Jesus is the "King of the world" of men. It is true of *His right* and true as a *prophecy*, but it is utterly untrue *in actual fact.* Our Lord was down here on earth *as prophet;* He is now up yonder in the holy place *as priest;* and one day, blessed be His Name! He is coming back to reign over the earth *as king.* But the kingdom is *not yet;* "The kingdom of (not *kingdoms)* the world is *not yet* become the kingdom of our Lord, and of His Christ." The evil one is yet "the god" and "the prince" of this world *(age).* He has his "headquarters of activity" in the upper spirit-realm that Paul calls "in the heavenlies," "in the air." Here he has a well organized army of subtle malignant evil spirits at his command. Paul calls them "principalities," "powers," "the world-rulers" of this "darkness," and "the powers of the air" among whom Satan is "prince."

The great object of this army of evil is to keep

possession of the hearts of men, and the New Testament narratives show clearly how obstinately they cling to such dwelling-places, and also that only the power of God can compel them to quit. As in the case of the demonized boy at the foot of the mount of transfiguration, the grip of some of these evil spirits upon their victims is such that only a *special faith* born of *special prayer* can cast them out. And they are cast out by Divine power, and in answer to persistent prayer. Some of them are less stubborn and their victims more easily won to God, but *prayer is needed for all.*

These being my convictions, and remembering how much of His time our Lord now spends in intercessory prayer, I give it *a large place* in my own life and work, and urge it above all things upon those with whom I toil. I ask them to put the mission into their prayers for weeks before I go among them. For a week before, I urge special prayer-meetings every night, and special subjects for prayer; such as, backsliders, unconverted seatholders, the unsaved in the sabbath-school, and the large army of absentees outside. This appeal for prayer I reiterate day by day during the mission, and give a marked place to silent prayer in every service. I also encourage and urge all the saved in my audiences to put in special requests for prayer on behalf of unsaved relatives and friends.

I very seldom preach a sermon on the first

Sunday morning of a mission. I find it better to outline the mission and my methods of working, and let the congregation know exactly the kind of results we seek. I expect prejudice in nearly every congregation, and try at the outset to remove it. There are usually a few seatholders present who have little or no sympathy with anything in the shape of a special mission. It may be that they cannot distinguish between dulness and death, and so mistake a dead formality for reverence. It may be that they have not enough personal religion to give them any sympathy with an earnest effort to lead others to seek it. Or it may be that in the past they have been repelled and disgusted by some pseudo-evangelist who has in their presence violated every canon of common sense and reverence in the pulpit, violated by forcing methods their free will, and loudly consigned them to the grotesque inferno of Tertullian, Dante, and mediæval Romanism. Such fears and prejudices I try at the beginning to clear away, and such people I thus try to win into sympathy with and attendance upon the mission.

Then I seek to show the Christians that the work is neither mine nor theirs but God's; that, in calling us to be His co-workers, He has put a wonderful honour upon us; that in His guidance and power we are His allies against the prince of evil and the forces that he leads and wields; and that the end of the fight is the winning of men "from the power of Satan

Quarry Beck, near Brampton. Mr. Waugh's Birthplace.

unto God." I show them by Scripture and illustration that the least and weakest among them has gifts to use and a sphere to fill, and that, if they have any share in the conflict and triumph, they will share in the gladness when up yonder we celebrate the victory in the "Harvest Home" of the skies. I encourage and cheer them by showing the importance of their work as compared with mine. I point out, not only how much I depend upon their prayers, but that if it were not for the work they have done in the past, much of my work would be impossible, and that if it were not for the work they will do when I am gone, much of my work would in the end count for nothing. So I seek to lead the church into a passion of saving sympathy and enthusiasm.

Then I let both the saved and the unsaved know that there will be *no teasing* in any shape or form. I have myself been so often shocked and hurt by this, that I cannot and will not have it in any of my meetings. I kindly but firmly let the workers know that if they begin that I shall close the mission and leave them. I am equally careful to let the unsaved know that they have nothing of that kind to fear. I justify my firmness in this matter by telling them of the pulling, hauling, badgering, and sometimes half-insulting I have seen done on these lines in mission services. The result is that in my missions nearly everyone present stays to the after-meetings. In nine missions out of ten there are people in the aisles and within the communion rail *during the prayer-meetings* at the close of the evening services.

Let me say at once that my references to this kind of badgering are made, not in any carping censorious spirit, but in all brotherly charity. I am ready to believe that in most cases, where this has been done, the motive has been the very highest; nevertheless I look upon it as being usually a grave error of judgment. A kindly word to one in apparent spiritual distress from one sitting near, or a sympathetic offer to accompany them into the inquiry-room, is often a great help to a timid one. Such offers of help I encourage on the last two or three nights of a mission. But that is entirely different from the wholesale prowling, surrounding, and teasing that have too often brought mission work into disrepute among thoughtful and reverent Christians, and done no end of harm to their victims. I believe that where one has been helped by such means nineteen have been spiritually hindered and injured.

At any rate, I am profoundly thankful that in the month I spent in feeling after God no one tried such methods with me. They would have done me no good, but a very great deal of harm. So, very kindly but earnestly, I tell the unsaved in my mission audiences that I am not going round among them cap in hand, asking them to bestow upon my Lord the favour of their patronage. There has been so much of this, that perverted human nature has taken a wrong view of the situation. Multitudes of people seem to think in these days that, if they get converted and join a church, both the Lord and the church ought to be very much obliged to them. The latter-day competition for church members has given them a half idea that the Lord cannot do without them. I always tell them in the opening service that the privilege is all on the other side. That God *can* do without them, though one day it will be terrible if they have to do without Him. I assure them that He will not violate their power of choice by forcing them into the fold, and we dare not and will not try.

Then again, I seek permanent results above all things else, and therefore set a high price upon unsaved people "counting the cost" before making a public decision for Christ. This is one reason why, as a rule, I do not formally open my inquiry rooms until the Wednesday night of the first week. Fifty thousand people at least, I believe, pray for me and my missions. In answer to these and to my own prayers there is an ever-deepening Divine power upon us in the meetings. Under that power, and the Divine light coming with it, I like the unsaved who need it to have a few days in which to think things over and try to see in what it will involve them to become Christ's men and women and to take a public stand for Him. I find that if they turn to God after such weighing of matters, there is little fear of their going back into the world.

When I was first led to this rule, it was a great test of my own faith and patience, and it is that still for many of my workers. Some earnest Christians, whose enthusiasm is years older than their spiritual judgment, find it hard to wait. They fairly hunger to decoy unsaved people forward by coming forward themselves with other Christians, and their hands and tongues fairly tingle to get at them in the pews and to fetch them out. While taking a firm stand, I try to be very patient and kindly with these eager ones, and before the mission closes they nearly always agree that *my way is best in my meetings.*

Because people are now more accustomed and therefore less susceptible to revival appeals than twenty years ago, it takes several days, in most cases, to lead them to ripeness for decision. To plead with them during the earlier nights, in long-drawn-out after-meetings, is a heavy strain on the faith of the workers, and often results in sinners coming out before the will and affections are set for Christ.

Of course I let them know that the door of the fold of God is open all the time. I urge them to immediate public decision, if they have already counted the cost. In order to help such I always, with a few workers, stay behind for a time, every night from the start of the mission. For similar reasons I never unduly prolong an after-meeting. I am afraid of their being persuaded to come out before they are really decided for Christ. I am often told that, if we continued another half-hour, more would come out, and I always point out that such almost-persuaded ones will form the *dry wood* with which to kindle the fire the next night. The longer I work on these lines, the more they commend themselves to me, though I would never dream of urging them upon any other missioner.

The thing to remember here is that sinners are like fruit, if picked before ripe they will not keep. In my meetings everything is made to lead to the first great end of the mission, the leading of men to God. With this in view the messages are prepared, the hymns chosen, and the prayers asked for and the theme suggested. Yet, if the decision be *only emotional*, and the reason and the will are not in it, it is no *real decision*. It is just here therefore where it pays grandly for the future, to be patient with the sinner and not hurry the work. From the pulpit I urge the unsaved not to leave their pews unless they are quite prepared to leave their sins. I assure them that God can never forgive the sin we will not give up. In such ways as these I do all I can to make the inquiry room work easy before the seekers enter it.

Then I advise my inquiry room helpers to work on similar lines, and not be in a hurry to "get them through." I believe that our Methodist forefathers, in their anxiety to have deep and permanent results, often allowed penitents to remain in spiritual distress far longer than was necessary. In these days the peril is the other way and we are too eager to get them to an *en masse* confession of Christ. The work is too much *on the surface*, and the value of *depth* is lost sight of. I look upon the inquiry room as the Holy of Holies in a mission, and ever urge its work as the most sacred and important, needing men and women of soul-touch and deep knowledge of the living word of God, and needing great prayerfulness and care.

I got a lesson in this, years ago, that I can never forget. In a mission in Scarborough a lot of stalwart Scotch fishermen were converted; among them a remarkable character for such a class and work. I just did have a task to get that man into the light. He argued and reasoned as if he was *all head* and yet I could see that he had a big heart and was desperately in earnest. I spent an hour per night for seven nights in personal dealing with that man; and then, late the last night, he fully trusted Jesus; five years later, I met him and most of those men saved with him, in the same chapel. Then they told me the man's story.

He had been educated for the Presbyterian ministry, and had gone through seven years of college training in Glasgow and Edinburgh. When the time for his ordination and taking a church came, he was too honest to occupy a false position. Rather than preach a gospel he had not himself accepted, he ran away to sea and lived a rough, sinful life. As soon as he was converted, he threw his whole soul into saving work, where, under the Spirit of God, his gifts and training at once made him a mighty power. Indoors or in the open air he always draws the crowd. As one of his mates said to me, "Whether by land or by sea, ever since his conversion he has been leading other people to Christ." When I heard this I was profoundly thankful that I had not begrudged the dear fellow any part of the seven hours I spent in personal dealing with him.

One other thing I have ever sought through all my public ministry has been *the winning of the men* for Christ. In most cases men are stronger than women, and thus the capture of the man usually means the winning of his wife and family. Then, too, women have more religious sense than men, and being more finely strung, more shut off from the world's distractions, and more thrown in upon themselves for the training of the children, they are generally more susceptible to the Christian evangel than the men.

Realising this, I have read, thought, and studied social and economic problems, specially to fit myself on the human side for getting hold of the men. As long as I was permitted to take three services per Sunday I nearly always had one for men only in the afternoons. Those meetings were the strength of my missions, and in scores of cases the victories were wonderful. And now I select most of my hymns with the men in view, and appeal as little as possible to the emotional, with will, head, and conscience left out. I appeal to their manliness, and show them what a manly thing the religion of Christ really is. And I always ask the inquirers to come into the room while we sing, while nearly everybody in the church can see them. This too appeals to the grit in them and calls it forth, for it takes some manly courage to come out in the presence of mates and friends like that.

Then again, I always accept the chance of speaking to bodies of working men in the dinner hour at or near large public works. This gets me among them; they cannot say we go *there* to "preach for money," and those meetings always bring a lot of them to my evening meetings. In my last Mission in Newcastle-on-Tyne, for instance, I addressed the men in different parts of the Elswick Works. The result was that two-thirds of my congregation were men, and nearly two-thirds of the inquirers, and a number of our very finest cases were men from those works. Similar results have followed in many other places where I have taken this course. Several years ago, when missioning in Portsmouth, I addressed over a hundred picked men on board the royal yacht, the "Victoria and Albert." A direct result was that eight of those men, four of their wives, and quite a number of their friends made a splendid public decision for Christ before my mission closed. I have at home, among my mementoes of God-given victories, a large framed photo of that yacht, that I prize more than I can say.

Need I say in closing this chapter on methods, that I always preach *the atonement* of Christ as *the ground of salvation* and of all the spiritual blessings we need and receive? As a bald theory to suit a certain type of mind, Unitarianism may be beautiful. As a saving system among guilty sinners, and as a dynamic in the midst of moral serfdom, it is as farcical as it is unscriptural. I do come into contact with it in *reasoning*, but I never hear of it *saving*. *It cannot save*, for "without shedding of blood there is no remission"; and, because it has no message or power to save, it is utterly discredited and useless as an evangel.

Tell the penitent thief he is to be saved by *the perfect example* of Christ, and with despair in his eyes and tones he will say, "Then I am lost. I have no time to study it for I am just about to die." Tell the penitent weeping Magdalene that she is to be saved by studying the *beautiful moral teachings* of Christ and receiving them into her heart, and she will say in utter hopelessness, "I dare not look at Him until I hear Him tell me I am forgiven." Thank God! we have a better gospel than that! A gospel full of hope and peace and cheer: "We have 'our' redemption through His blood, the forgiveness of our sins."

CHAPTER VIII.

The First Essential.

IN this and in several succeeding chapters I propose to put before my readers a few of the most important lessons in Christian work, that I have learned in my long experience as an evangelist. And the lesson I learned at college, the lesson burned in upon me more deeply than any other ever since, is this: *The first great factor in the saving of men is* THE POWER, *the Spirit of God.*

At first sight, one of the most perplexing things in our Lord's early ministry was its brevity. He was down here among men for a little over thirty years, and, as far as we know, He only spent a trifle over three years of that time in active ministry. No one knew as He knew how ripe the times had become for what He had to say and do. No one understood as He did the deep pathetic widespread need for His message and His ministry. Yet He never opened His mouth or lifted His hand in that ministry, until He received His great equipment for it in the fulness of the Holy Spirit.

We read that when He came up out of the

Jordan from His baptism, the voice of the Father was heard, speaking of Him in words of warm approval, and the Holy Spirit was seen falling upon Him in the form of a dove. It was not in that form that that same Spirit came to the disciples some three years later. He came upon them in the form of "tongues of fire," and we can understand the difference. *They* had sin to burn out, and *the fire* was needed. "He knew no sin," and so the Spirit of God fell upon Him under the symbol of peace.

Now that He has received His great qualification for it, our Lord at once enters upon His ministry, and the first phase of it awaiting Him was *temptation*. If in the coming age He was to understand and succour His trusting ones when tempted, He Himself "must suffer being tempted." Hence we read that right away from the Jordan, "Jesus, full of the Holy Spirit, was led by the Spirit into the wilderness" "to be tempted." Here He was for forty days in terrible conflict with the leader of the hosts of darkness. It was in the fulness of the Spirit's power that Jesus entered that conflict, and in that power, using the word He had given, He got the victory. If you and I, my reader, get into that wilderness and meet that same tempter, if it be this same Holy Spirit who leads us there, He will stay there with us until He has given us the victory too.

The evil one conquered, "Jesus returned in the power of the Spirit into Galilee." On the sabbath day "He entered, as His custom was, the synagogue." When the time for the lesson arrived, the roll of the prophet Isaiah was handed to Him to read the portion for the day, and the first words He read were these; "The Spirit of the Lord is upon Me because He anointed Me *to preach.*" After a few more sentences, He closed the roll and handed it back to the attendant, saying, "To-day hath this scripture been fulfilled in your ears." Now, strictly speaking, Christ did not come into the world to preach the gospel, but rather that there might be a gospel to preach. Nevertheless He had a message, a wonderful message it was, and a wonderful power He had in delivering it. How the common people crowded to hear Him and hung on His words! How mightily, yet how differently, His hearers were moved by His words! How marvellously the world is being moved by those words to-day! They rang out from those grassy pulpits on Judæan hillsides, or from the deck of a boat by the shore of Galilee's lake, and they are ringing in men's ears and hearts still. They have rolled down through the centuries, gathering power as they have come, until they have been listened to by every nation on the face of the earth. And the great secret of our Lord's power in speech was this, "the Spirit of the Lord" was upon Him. Aye, my reader, and that has been the great secret of all effective speech for God among men ever since.

But our Lord had a ministry *of work* as well as

of speech, a blessed ministry of deeds as well as of words. More than three years after this, Peter opened the door of the kingdom to the Gentiles at Cæsarea. In his address to Cornelius and his household he tells us that "God anointed Jesus of Nazareth" "with the Holy Ghost and with power," that is, with the power of the Holy Ghost. And what next? What would we expect to follow such a statement, but the words we find?—"Who went about doing good." Filled with this fulness, we cannot do other, it is then our very nature, our very life, to go about doing good.

One lovely evening in last May, my host and I had a two hours' walk through the fields and woods near Glastonbury in Somerset. The smaller songsters had gone to rest, but with the larger birds it was evensong. We heard dozens of thrushes with their cheery notes, and blackbirds with their mellow flute-like tones. There was plenty of bass too, for again and again we heard the hoarse croak of the cock pheasant, the call of the partridge, and the resonant notes of the cuckoo. In that walk, too, we heard six different nightingales and saw three of them. I never listened to such a choir in my life, and there was not a paid member among them. They sang because they could not help it. God had put the music in their souls, and it was bound to come out, and it did, to their evident delight and ours.

It is just the same in the service of God and

humanity. Filled with the Holy Spirit, we cannot but go about doing good. If we are invalids and cannot "go about," then people will come to us, as they went to Paul in prison, to receive the good. It was thus with our Lord. When He gave sight to the blind, speech to the dumb, hearing to the deaf, power to the palsied, activity to the crippled, and life to the dead, this was the secret of His might. And when He turned out evil spirits from the hearts of those whom they had degraded and cursed, it was in the same power, for He said, "I by the Spirit of God cast out devils."

So those wonderful three years of active ministry ended, and our Lord entered upon the passive phase of His mission on earth. The shadows of Gethsemane and Golgotha had been upon Him all the way through, becoming darker and more dreadful as He neared them, and now they are upon Him. In the garden He is crushed with the weight of a world's sin, until the grass under Him is wet with the dew of His anguish. Behind the garden there is the cross with its pain and shame, with its bitterest of all the consequences of man's sin;—separation from the Father. What that meant to His pure spirit we may never fathom, but we get some hint of it in His heartbroken cry, "My God! My God! why hast Thou forsaken Me?" And, dear reader, let me write it very reverently, He entered and went through that awful passion, and offered that great atonement for human sin, in the power through which He had wrought His active ministry. The writer of the epistle to the Hebrews tells us that Jesus "through the Eternal Spirit offered Himself without spot to God." And when a few weeks later He left His disciples on the side of Olivet, it was "through the Holy Spirit" that He gave them His final commandments and their world-wide commission in the gospel. From first to last, for every part of His ministry, our Lord's great qualification was the fulness of the Holy Spirit.

Now let us turn from the Master to His messengers. On the evening of His resurrection day, the disciples, for fear of the Jews, were met in secret. They had probably all visited or at least heard of their Lord's vacant tomb, and were discussing the wondrous event, when He Himself appeared in their midst. After a word of greeting in the form of a word of peace, He said to them, "*As* My Father hath sent Me, even *so* send I you." The "as" was a look back to the Jordan, and the "so" a look forward to pentecost. The "as" referred to the way in which the Father had sent Him, and the "so" to the way in which He would send them. We have seen that the Father sent Him by filling Him with the Holy Spirit, and in exactly the same might He will send them. Hence we read that "He breathed on them," and—in prophecy and promise of pentecost—said, "Receive ye the Holy Ghost."

When, a few weeks afterwards, He was taken away from them, they returned to Jerusalem, and it is instructive to note how loyally they obeyed His injunctions about their mission and their fitness for it. Dim as their knowledge yet was, none knew as they knew the meaning of the message they were to deliver. None could feel as they did the need of that great city being crowded for the coming passover, and of the great world beyond, yet their lips were silent except to God in prayer. Following the example and command of their Master, they did not touch their ministry until the qualifying power had come to them. For ten days they left men in their need, for persistent expectant prayer to God.

The tenth day came, and with it the promised baptism of fire. And what a morning it was! The birthday of the Christian church and the day of her anointing for her mission! And what a morning for the world! Before the shades of night had thickened down upon Jerusalem three thousand people had left its ranks for the fold of Christ. Thank God! That fulness then given to the church has *never been withdrawn.* For nearly twenty years I have urged this on my hearers. No need to pray now for "an outpouring of the Holy Spirit." He was that morning "poured out" by the risen Lord, and He is here in His church still. It is not "outpouring" on God's part that is needed, but *inletting* on ours. If the church would risk His searching fire and accept the conditions, He is longing to fill her even now. No need for us to "wait" if willing to be filled. They had to wait till Jesus was "glorified," for then in New Testament fulness the promised Paraclete had not come; but that day He came to His own, and for His fulness we need not "wait," but *trust* and *receive.*

What a start He gave the work, to be sure! Three thousand people turned to God in one day, through the ministry of a few Galilean fishermen and their lowly fellow-Christians! In a few days the numbers rolled up to twenty thousand, as Luke's figures show when we allow for the usual proportion of women. This, of course, the devil and the priests did not like, and a bitter persecution broke out against the followers of the crucified Messiah. That persecution became so cruel and relentless that finally it scattered the young church into all the regions round about. But that did not stay the tide of Christian conquest. It simply turned the members of the church into missionaries who carried the gospel with tongues of flame wherever they went. So everywhere the tide of victory went with them, turning their toil and sorrow into joy.

Do I need to tell my readers that pagan priests met Christianity with hatred and opposition, as did the Jewish priests in Jerusalem? Do I need to tell them that pagan emperors for three centuries sought to drown out the young church in the blood of her own martyrdom? But I can tell them that it was all in vain. The cruelty of the persecution was not more marked than the fortitude of its victims. This world has never known more sublime heroism than that of those early Christian martyrs. Multitudes of them were but girls and lads of tender years. As one reads the terrible but glorious story, the tears spring, but one's faith and courage are nerved and braced at the same time. Filled with the Holy Spirit, death had no terrors for them, and torture was but a rough road to a martyr's crown. With God's light in their eyes, and Zion's songs on their lips, they walked to arena, stake, or block as to their coronation. The more they were persecuted the more they multiplied. The red rain of their martyr blood but enriched the ground for the growing of grander Christian harvests. The victories they won were such that in three hundred years, all over Asia, on the southern fringe of Europe, and on the Northern and Eastern sea-boards of Africa, paganism was tottering to its fall.

In the morning of the fourth century the emperor Constantine realised that persecution could neither save paganism nor destroy Christianity, and he took another course. He met the church with a smile instead of a frown. He offered her the hand of friendship instead of the sword of persecution, and the new method succeeded. The church was blinded and deceived, and made her first great mistake.

As long as she was loyal to her commission; as long as she expected Divine results only from Divine power; as long as her reliance upon the guidance and power of the Holy Spirit was absolute—she was almost irresistible. But the smile of the world did what its persecutions had failed to do, and the church fell into the snare. She largely transferred her dependence from Divine power to the smile of royalty and the patronage of a throne. She forgot the simplicity of Christ in the blandishments of earthly place and power. Her pastors, true bishops already, swelled up into prelates, and her prelates budded into princes. Then the princes of the Church began to vie with the princes of the State in dress, in equipage, in home, in luxury, and in the pomp and pride of life. Then the real victories of the church almost ceased. From that time she steadily drifted into the deep darkness and superstition of the Middle Ages, from which she was only partly roused through the trumpet voice of Martin Luther and his fellow-reformers.

It has been the same ever since, and it is the same to-day. As the church is Spirit-filled her work is fruit-filled, as she is God-possessed herself she is God-blessed to others, and here we may find the secret of much of her impotence and failure during the last twenty years. We have in this land to-day a fine army of gifted ministers, and a still mightier army of lay toilers. We have a wonderfully powerful and flexible set of ecclesiastical machinery, and unparalleled resources are placed at our disposal by our present-day civilization. The churches are wealthy as never before and as a result, churches, chapels, mission halls and rooms, sabbath-schools and other church premises are multiplying at a marvellous rate. But are they all fulfilling their end? Are the real results commensurate with the cost and activity? I wish I could say "Yes," but I dare not. I am not blind to nor unthankful for the signs of the times during the last twelve months, and I am eagerly expecting better days. But, as yet, the discrepancy between the resources and possibilities of the Christian church on one side, and the saving of the people on the other, is heart-breaking.

The nostrums recommended in order to secure greater success are legion, and most of them are urged by great and good men. One suggests shorter sermons, another a more liturgical service, and yet another the very opposite. In the long list of recipes for the greater success of the work, we have—no pew rents, democratic church polity, the institutional church, and more open-air preaching.

There is something in all these suggestions. They are all worthy of consideration and are not to be dismissed by a wave of the hand. But not one of them goes to the root of the thing. They are all suggestions about *machinery* and methods, while *the greatest need* is *more power.* We have more machinery already than we have power to drive, and hence the added power, the so urgently needed power, must be our first care.

I am so certain about this that I increasingly feel it to be the first need of the church of God in these latter days. However commodious and suitable, our churches, chapels, sabbath-schools, mission halls and kindred ecclesiastical buildings: however gifted, scholarly, well-read and eloquent, our ministers and lay preachers: however intelligent, earnest, and well-informed, our staff of sabbath-school teachers: however level-headed common-sense and business-like, our stewards, elders and deacons: however highly gifted and well trained, our organists and choirs: however wise, strong and elastic the connections between the church and the people she is sent to save: whatever we may have of material machinery or human agency,—*it is only powerful to save men and women, as it is guided and empowered by the Spirit of God.* Only Divine power can achieve Divine results, and saving work is Divine.

Take the revival in Wales as an illustration of this. I believe in special missions, planned and arranged for, and worked on business-like methodical lines. I know that good and earnest men, in view of the work in Wales, have pleaded that "we do not want a mission but a revival." That sounds both reverent and clever, but there is more of human smartness than spiritual sense in it. God has so often made "a mission" the starting point or occasion of "a revival," that the above plea has no meaning. Nevertheless I am thankful that in the whole of the glorious work in Wales there has hardly been anything like a regular mission, and that the most marked method has been the absence of any method at all. I believe that "evangelists" are called of God for the special work of missioning, and I believe that to be my own calling, yet I do rejoice that in this blessed work in Wales all the well-known evangelists have been passed over, and the Holy Spirit has mostly used a lot of men, women, lads and girls who were never heard of before. It shows all the more clearly that *the work is of God.* The blessed Spirit works through missioners and missions, but apart from them as well, and therein we evangelists do most heartily rejoice.

That is, the first great factor in the saving of men is *the power, the Spirit of God.* I have never heard of, read of, or known at any time in any place, any man, woman, youth or maiden being converted to God, except by the Spirit of God. Whatever human and mechanical agencies may have been used in saving, *He has used them.* He only can show the need for, make willing to receive, and then impart, the new life, in the new birth. Every soul born into the circle of the saved must be "born of the Spirit."

CHAPTER IX.

The Next Essentials.

GUIDED and empowered by the Spirit of God, the second great factor in the saving of men, is THE AGENT, *the man or woman of God.* I have never heard nor read of, I have never known a case at any time in any place, of any man, woman, youth, or maiden being converted to God by the Spirit of God, *without His using some man or woman of God, or more, in one way or another in leading to their conversion.* It was to *men* that our Lord said, "So send I you"; "Go ye into all the world and preach the gospel"; and, "Ye are My witnesses." That little commissioned circle of Christ-lovers was wonderfully widened a little later, and from that time until now God has ever had in the world an apostolic succession of Spirit-possessed men and women, through whom He has been reaching and saving other men and women. And believe me, my reader, there is no other apostolic succession worth the name.

One of the most important questions we are ever asked in these days is this;—"Is salvation possible outside the church?" Limiting the word "salvation" to its strictly gospel meaning, and excluding its meanings as applied to the Hebrew, and to the heathen at home and abroad, I always answer "No." Of course by "the church" I do not mean "the churches" as denominations, but the true "body of Christ" made up of those who are "joined to the Lord" by a living faith and thus "made partakers of the Divine nature." The churches may be the best method we yet have of measuring the place and progress of the church, but the two words are not synonymous. The Christian church is to be the visible expression, the present manifestation to the world, of the risen Christ. But too often the churches *mis*represent instead of representing their Lord.

Then again, though less and narrower, the church is greater and wider than the churches, because there are members of the church who are—generally to their loss—outside all the churches. Yet many of these good souls have the Lord's cause at heart and do some real saving work. One of the most interesting results of the impetus given to aggressive Christian effort by the glorious revival begun under the ministry of Moody and Sankey in 1873 is the widespread multiplication of more or less *free-lance evangelism.* Multitudes of earnest souls, sick of dull dreariness in churches, and pained at the sight of churches and ministers that neither save nor care to save the perishing, struck out on mission lines of their own. Mission halls and rooms became the order of the day, and have continued to be. Of course the real purpose of such missions has often been caricatured, and many of these places have become veritable caves of Adullam. Many of them, more or less loosely connected with some church, have nearly driven the minister and officials out of their minds. Nevertheless, a great deal of the finest saving work done in this land for years has been done under just such conditions as these. Scores of undenominational places like the Star Hall in Ancoats, the Assembly Hall in Mile End Road, and the Centenary Hall in Stratford, have for years been the birthplace for God of multitudes of souls. Similar blessings too have been given of God in foreign lands through the Mildmay, the Grattan Guinness, and the China Inland Missions, and through the Students' Voluntary Medical Missionary Union. But, if outside the churches, these missions and missioners, at home and abroad, are *all in the church.*

A keen piquancy is given to this question by the present-day system of permitting non-christian men and women to take part in Christian work. It is no breach of the law of Christian charity to say that there are hundreds of unsaved men in the pulpits of this and other lands. There are multitudes of unregenerate men and women at our organs, in our choirs, teaching in our sabbath-schools, and holding offices in the churches. On moral grounds we have no word to say against them, but mere morality and musical teaching, or business gifts, are not New Testament qualifications for office or work in the church of Christ. Then it is quite a common thing to invite members of the aristocracy and civic dignitaries to open churches, schools, and bazaars, without a question about their moral character, to say nothing of their being the Lord's people or not. And, perhaps worse still, ministers and laymen alike often invite to be chairmen of meetings, or go for subscriptions to, men who are known to be utterly godless, and some of whom have made their wealth out of the oppression or ruin of their fellow-men.

Though it is a modern one, this is certainly not the apostolic method. The rule then was that only spiritual men must touch spiritual work, only those *in Christ* were allowed to toil for Christ, and this was the will and plan of the Lord who sent them. His "go ye" was only to *His own*, and only His own are ever called to and sent in His service. He may overrule and use the words and works of unsaved people in the furtherance of His cause, but the great New Testament principle is:—*that only members of the church of Christ can do the work of Christ.* We must come to Him before we can work for Him. We must know Him before we can lead others to Him. We must have His life before we can do His will.

We must be saved ourselves if we are to be used in saving others. It may sound a bit keen and searching, but our Lord's meaning is unmistakable when He tells us that when He comes He will be compelled to say "I never knew you" to people who have "cast out devils" in His name "and in His name done many wonderful works."

As it is only through His own that God does His saving work, the work *will not be done unless they do it.* He will go *with* them and make their message a saving message, but not *without* them. As I have a chapter on the subject in my "Sonship and Service," I need not here try to show again that Christ as "the head of the body, which is the church," is dependent upon the members of His body for carrying out His will and purposes. It was significant of this, when, in promising the Paraclete to His disciples, our Lord said, "I will send Him *unto you*, and He, when He is come, He will *convict the world*." How literally too this was fulfilled at Pentecost! It was not upon the crowd in the streets that the Holy Spirit fell in tongues of flame, but upon the interceding saints in the upper room. Then, *through them* and their ministry He reached and saved the willing ones in the crowd outside.

When in some churches we preach this truth, cold and lazy church members strongly resent it. We hear of them saying: "I don't like that kind of preaching, it does not help or comfort me. I don't care for men who preach so much about Christian responsibility and work. The saving of men is God's work and He will do it." I solemnly say that "*He will not* do it apart from saved human instrumentality." I cannot find any hint in the New Testament of God saving any single person apart from the sympathy, prayer, and co-operation of His people. He might have saved that eunuch and made him a messenger of Christ to his dark-skinned brethren in Ethiopia, without calling Philip away from his grand mission work in Samaria; but He did not. He could, I reckon, have led Cornelius and his household into the fold of Christ, without giving those messengers that walk to Joppa, Peter his vision, and Peter and the men the journey back to Cæsarea; but it was not His way. Always the human agent.

Of course I believe that God might have chosen to save men in some other way; but He has not, and I for one am thankful that He has not. I am glad that in choosing the heralds of this salvation God has passed by angels and all other possible ministries, and conferred the honour upon saved men and women. It is a terrible responsibility, a solemn truth, but I for one joyously welcome it. It means filling up "that which is behind of the afflictions of Christ." It means soul-burden, travail of spirit, intense intercession, hard work, sacrifice and tears, but like Paul, "I rejoice" in it with a great joy. I am more thankful than words can tell that we reclaimed sinners are the way back to God for those who are still wandering. It gives you and me a share, my reader, in the grandest work on earth. It makes us "co-workers together with God." Fancy *that* for unworthy you and me! It gives us a share in the work which is more to God and all heaven than any other work on earth. It gives us the joy and honour of giving our dear Lord *His greatest joy*, the joy of saving, the joy that is His sweet recompence for "the travail of His soul."

The longer I am in and study Christian work, the more I am persuaded that, as a rule, no one knows who, humanly speaking, has the most to do with any one person's conversion. I honestly believe that in this age multitudes have been converted, with whom in each case God has used scores of different Christians in leading up to the final surrender to Christ. Aye, and it is just wonderful how He can bring in the different agents at the right time and make their work part of a grandly successful plan. Let me give a personal illustration that I have given elsewhere, and which I repeat here at the request of many to whom it has been a help.

On the last night of a mission I held in Bolton, a few years ago, I asked the audience to pray specially for a cousin of mine, living in a Cheshire village six miles from Chester and twelve from Liverpool. He bore my own name, had a wife and family of children, and was drifting deeply into the grip of strong drink. He had been greatly impressed in one of my meetings in Cockermouth seven years before this, and I wanted him under my message again.

On the Sunday after the mission in Bolton I was to preach in Brunswick chapel, Liverpool, so I told the audience of my cousin, and asked them to pray that, wherever he might be on the following sabbath, the Holy Spirit might arrest him, bring him to Liverpool to my service and save him before he left. They did pray too, and God did gloriously answer them.

At noon that Sunday, Tom Waugh was standing outside the village public-house waiting for it to open. Just then, the Lord sent along a Primitive Methodist who knew him, and who told him he had no business there that day. Then he told him I was to preach in Liverpool and in which chapel. Tom went in and had his beer and then went home to dinner. His wife had seen him enter the drink-shop, and he saw that she had been in tears.

The mention of my name and proximity had brought memories that impressed him, and the sight of his wife's tears deepened that impression. He got up from the table and said, "Helen, I'm going to Liverpool to hear my cousin Tom preach." She replied, "You cannot get there now, Tom." Saying "But I *will* get there," the dear fellow set off to walk the twelve miles, to hear me. When he had walked half way, the Lord sent along three local preachers in a trap, on their way to their afternoon appointments. One of them knew my cousin and asked him where he was going. On hearing his reply, he said, "Why, you are just in time to catch a train at Ledsham, and it will save you a walk of six miles." Tom caught the train for Birkenhead, and after a wash and cup of tea, found his way across to Bıunswick chapel, Liverpool.

When I reached the chapel vestry a few minutes before service time, I was told that he was in an adjoining room and wanted to see me. After a few words with him I asked one of the officials to take him up to a seat in the chapel, which was already packed into the aisles. I told the other officials in the vestry of my request at Bolton, of my own prayers, of my belief that Tom would be saved that night, and asked them to join me in intercession for him.

Though the chapel was packed to the rostrum, the man who took my cousin up into the chapel saw room for one at the end of a seat in the gallery. That steward did not know it, but the Lord had specially reserved that seat for his charge. The man did not know it then, but he set Tom next to a man who had known him, and whom he had known since they went to school and played together when lads at home. That man had been saved two years before in one of my meetings in Brunswick, and was just eager to win others to Christ.

When, from the rostrum, I saw where the Lord had seated my cousin, I felt sure he would be one of the first to decide for Christ that night, and my faith was not disappointed. The moment I gave the invitation in the after-meeting, Tom was the first of over thirty to come out publicly seeking Jesus. His old playmate came with him and showed him the way, and soon they rejoiced together. After my word of congratulation and advice, Tom had supper with his friend and then walked the twelve miles home. He arrived at two o'clock and found the wife waiting up for him. When she heard the glad news of his conversion she wisely saw that they must be as one in this thing. They began a prayer-meeting together, and she found the Lord at her own fireside. Since then the elder children have turned to Christ, and since then the minister in charge of the Primitive Methodist chapel there has told me that my cousin's conversion was the starting-point of a beautiful revival of God's work in the place.

Only the Lord could have called in all those different human instrumentalities and made them form such a beautiful sequence, leading to such grand results. Always the agent, the man or woman of God, used by the Spirit of God in bringing others to God. Christ alone can save men, but according to His revealed plan He cannot save them alone. "Channels only," but *channels needed*, and channels used as unimpeded. All saved people are thus responsible for the salvation of others, according to their gifts and opportunities. We are saved to save, and by lip and pen, in one way or another, as well as by fervent and persistent prayer, we can all do something to hasten the triumph of our coming King. Those who claim to be saved but do nothing for the saving of others are incurring a grave risk before God. They are disloyal to the saving plan of the Lord whose name they bear, and are frustrating His glorious saving purposes for others through them.

The third great essential in the saving of men is THE MEDIUM, *the word of God.* I have never heard nor read of, I have never known a case at any time in any place, of any man, woman, youth, or maiden being converted to God by the Spirit of God, *without the word of God being used in one way or another in leading to their conversion.* "Of His own will begat He us with *the word of truth,*" says James, and to the same effect is the word in Peter, "We are born—the second time—not of corruptible, but of incorruptible seed, of *the word of God.*" The saving work of the Holy Spirit is always *through* the human agent and *by* the Divine word. "He shall take of Mine," said the Lord; and from that time until now He has been using "the truth as it is in Jesus," alike in converting sinners and sanctifying saints.

In the New Testament the Holy Spirit is called "the hand of the Lord," and the word of God is called "the sword of the Spirit." How well these figures agree! How splendidly a hand and a sword fit each other in conflict! Without the hand to wield it the sword is powerless, and without His sword the life-giving Spirit cannot reach and pierce the heart of the sinner He is seeking to save. There must be *saving truth* as well as the *saving Spirit* in the saving of men. The ambassadors of Christ are sent to "preach the word," and it is through "the foolishness of preaching" that God saves "those who believe."

The longer I am an evangelist, the more I realise the important place of the word of God in saving work, and the more I urge it upon our people. We are often told that "there has not been much preaching in connection with the revival in Wales." In a surface sense that seems to be true, but in the true sense it is a mistaken view. The whole of the Welsh revival area is studded with churches, chapels, sabbath-schools, and Christian missions. Inside or under the influences of these places and their message nearly all the converts of the revival have been reared, and the saving truths of the gospel were already in them. Those truths have been appealed to by the Holy Spirit, waked up into active operation, and used in saving these people. Then too the prayers, the testimonies, and the appeals of the movement have been shot through and through with gospel texts and truths, and this is one of the factors accounting for the blessed permanence of the results.

Believing this in my heart, I often declare in public that one of our most glaring weaknesses as a church is our widespread and often pitiful ignorance of the word of God. I am ashamed again and again of that ignorance, and often in a big church with a big membership we cannot find a dozen people who can sit down with their Bibles and intelligently point broken-hearted sinners to Christ.

The longer I preach, the more earnestly I seek a verdict for Christ *while I am preaching*, and expect the people to give it. For this I pray, and for this I look and plead more than ever; and the result is that more and more I find that people are saved while I preach. In nearly every mission people tell the inquiry-room workers that they got saved under the sermon, and people are constantly telling me in these days that while I was delivering some sermon or lecture they were led into saving fellowship with Christ. A short time ago, at the close of a sermon, two married couples and a young man walked up to the pastor of the church and told him they had found peace under the sermon, and all of them through one simple scriptural illustration. Not long ago two young ladies and their brother were all saved in a pew in a Plymouth chapel, during my sermon, and two fine young men in Nottingham told me they had trusted Christ whilst I was lecturing on "Manliness." And only last Monday night a young married couple and two young men stood up in my service and told us they had been saved at home, after the previous evening's service.

For similar reasons I urge a careful use of the Scriptures upon my mission helpers, especially upon those who have to deal with inquirers, and at the close of the meeting I give them a short address on the last steps to the cross. Illustrations and passages from the word of God are here far more effective than any words of men, and it is a joy to see so often, the new light of vision and acceptance leap into the eyes of seekers for God, even while we speak.

CHAPTER X.

Revivals and the Churches.

IN my handbook on "Special Missions" I have so fully discussed the place of mission work in the churches, and its relations to the work of the regular pastorate, that I do not propose to deal with it in this volume at all. But I have in these years learnt a few lessons as to *the value of revivals to the churches and to the community*, which I may with profit to my readers state in this and the following chapter.

The very word "revival" means a *quickening and deepening of life already possessed.* This means that the church herself is the earthly starting point of every true revival. She has life, spiritual life, already. That life she has from her risen Head Jesus Christ, by the operation of the Holy Spirit He has sent to indwell her as His body. But life spiritual, like life physical, may be possessed in wonderfully varying degrees, and a revival in a church means that the members receive "life *more abundantly*." As the Holy Spirit is the imparter of this life, it follows that a church has life just in proportion as she is possessed by the Holy Spirit. Every revival therefore is and must be first and foremost the work of the Spirit of God. But the very first "fruit of the Spirit is *love*," and thence when "filled with the Spirit" we are filled with love. Let us now try to see what this mostly means to a Christian church.

And first of all a real revival largely *settles the question of sin.* A church is made up of individuals, and *love for a person* is the very soul of the Christian religion. The members filled with love means a love-filled church, and as we love Christ we get rid of everything in our lives that we know can grieve Him and injure His cause.

Love is the secret of happy wedded life. Living in the close and sacred marriage bond, husband and wife find out each other's likes and dislikes, and what things in their dispositions and characters give pleasure to or hurt each other. We always seek to give joy to those we love and to avoid the things that give them pain. Thus loving, man and wife seek to conquer what grieves and to cultivate what gives joy to each other, and in this way they become truly one in heart and character.

Just as we love our Lord we shun the things that He most dislikes and hates, and thus above all things we seek to be done with sin. We know something of what sin cost Him, and of how it crucifies

Him afresh, and we fear to pain Him whom we love and to whom we owe so much.

How clearly this is illustrated in the conduct of the disciples before and after pentecost! Before their baptism of fire they, though followers of Christ, were full of the unworthy weaknesses and tempers that are so sadly common among professed disciples of Christ in these days. They were filled with unbelief, cowardice, and selfishness, and with the most childish personal ambitions. They wrangled with each other about honours and front seats in the coming kingdom. John and James, through their mother, wanted to reserve for themselves the seats next to the Lord Himself in that kingdom. And how narrow and intolerant were those brothers! When a Samaritan village refused to receive their Master, they wanted to play Elijah out of Elijah's times, and call down fire upon those deluded villagers.

But what a change after the tongues of flame reached them! Their ambitions for personal place and honour became ambitions for the honour and cause of their Lord. Their longings for their own advancement and fancies became longings for the saving of their fellow-men. Not the flame of death but the word of life they then longed to take into Samaria. Bickerings and jealousies perished in the glow of a new-born love that became the special mark of the church of God.

Will my readers specially note that this deliverance from selfish ambitions, petty jealousies, and unmanly cowardice came *after* and not *before* Pentecost? I would be one of the last to minimise in any way the unspeakable privilege of these men in having had three years of personal fellowship with Christ. To walk with Him, to commune with Him, to listen to His words, and through them and His gracious healing deeds to see into His heart of love, must have been a wondrous privilege and joy. To be under the stimulus of His matchless example, to listen to His counsels and teachings, and to enter somewhat into His gracious purposes, must have been a rare opportunity and honour.

And yet the unchristlike tempers, attitudes, and ambitions, and the pitiful ignorances of these men, were with and in them at the close of those three wonderful years. There never were such teachings and example as those of Christ, and we cannot be too thankful for them; but it was not these, but the pentecostal flame, that made these men anew. There is nothing like fire for destroying rubbish, and these very faulty followers of Christ were that day made into new men. "The fruit of the Spirit is *love*," and after this they loved their Lord as never before. The Holy Spirit now *filling* them interpreted for them more fully the example Jesus had set them and the teachings He had given them. He made them hunger to reach that incomparable likeness, and gave them a fuller power by which they might attain to it.

Is not this, a revival of spiritual life by the Holy Spirit, exactly what most churches need to-day? I know something of our Lord's love for His church, and I have no sympathy with parading her faults and holding them up to ridicule in the presence of her enemies. There is no more pitiful mistake made in the pulpit than when men seek to win the applause of the crowd by scourging the churches in their presence. But is there not in multitudes of churches enough of pre-pentecostal unchristlike life to make our hearts ache and to bring the tears to our eyes?

One cannot wonder that many churches are paralysed and do practically nothing for Christ. In some of them the ladies set the fashions for the neighbourhood, and worship the world in the house of the Lord it rejects. Some are ruled and filled with the pride of caste and social cliques, and if the poor man of James ii. 2, were to come in once, it would be his last visit there. Some are the one-man-show of some wealthy nabob who worships himself in the house of God. The church must walk in his boots, and because the boots are too small she cannot walk at all. Some churches are the special Sunday domain of a few families who are united by marriage or business and to whom all else must bow. Others are full of family feuds and bitter heart-burnings and jealousies, where they love each so much they would almost rather die than speak to each other. In others there are debtors who can but will not pay their debts, and others who put money into God's plate on Sundays that they take out of the devil's hands on all the other days. In some churches there are men in office and power whose lives are a disgrace to society, to say nothing of a Christian church ; while in others, for the sake of their position and money, men are tolerated in office, whose selfish imperious wills and violent tempers often turn church meetings into bear-gardens or earthly pandemoniums.

It is heart-breaking, but these things are sad facts, and have a sad effect upon "those that are without." Many of these churches are constant objects of the well-earned contempt and scorn of the ungodly within their reach. Others, that are free from these gross inconsistencies, are cold, dead, and powerless to save. False pride and an equally false respectability freeze everything in the place. The man in the pulpit is selected and paid to keep them up in current events, and to comfort them in the thought that a Sunday decorum in a Christian church is a true mark of their being Christians. Anything in the shape of spiritual stirrings on God's part and spiritual distress on man's part would be a fearful violation of the canons of their church life, and must be rigorously excluded.

These are Christian churches *in name only*, and nothing but a spiritual revival by the Holy Spirit can make them such *in fact.* We have known scores such, the life of whose members made them a laughing-stock before godless men. In answer to the intercessions of a faithful spiritual few, they were visited of the Holy Ghost, the members were caught in the holy fire and made anew, and now those churches are a "savour of Christ" and a saving power among the people. We have known churches noted for their cold dead formality, that have been visited and set on a blaze in the same way, and ever since their fiery chrism they have been filled with a passionate ambition to rescue the perishing around them. Such revivals the Lord has often granted in connection with my own missions, and with those of men who in this and other lands are called to similar toil. Only a revival can save such churches, for it is the fulness of love inwrought by the Holy Spirit that settles the question of actual sin, and of the laziness and neglect of the perishing that in themselves are a sin against God and men.

Then again, a revival *settles the question of worldliness.* From the very beginning, the principles of the church and those of the world—the world of unbelief in Christ, the world that rejects Him—have ever been in direct antagonism. There can be no mistake about the declarations of the word of God in this matter. "Friendship with the world is enmity against God," and, "If any man love the world the love of the Father is not in Him," are statements needing no explanations. The world hated the Christ, and in its heart still hates His claims, principles, and cross. Its aims are all on earth and the church's highest aims are in heaven. It is of the earth earthy, and the church is of heaven, heavenly. The measure of the church's distance from the world in aims, maxims, principles, ambitions, pursuits, pleasures, and purposes, has ever been the measure of her being well-pleasing to God and a blessing to men. The measure of her oneness with the world has ever been the measure of her disloyalty to God, and of her unfitness and powerlessness for her mission to humanity.

And in these latter years the worldliness of the churches has been their greatest bane. The world smiles on the church to-day and the church crosses over to the world in the light of the smile. The professed friendship of the world and the acceptance of it by the church have done more to secularize her and rob her of her power to save and bless than the bitterest persecution could ever have done. The union of the two is in these days so close, that the mission of the one and the need and doom of the other are largely forgotten. Their walks and interests are so closely blended, and the imitation of the world by the church is so close and constant, that in many cases they cannot be distinguished.

We wonder that the unsaved largely keep outside the churches; but if they see no difference between those outside and those inside, except in a few formal Sunday customs and forms, what can we expect? The shrewdest Christian cannot tell in these days where the church ends and the world begins, nor see any difference in principles, character and life-work between the bottom lot in the church and the top lot in the world. In too many cases there is no difference that can be felt or seen, and hence the church does not impress the world with its own needs and the Lord's calls and claims. The world has largely conquered the church instead of the church conquering the world. The world sees no need of coming into the church, because the church goes into the world for companionship, amusement, pleasure and gain.

The great cure for this is a spiritual revival. Let the church get Spirit-filled, and she is at once world-emptied. With a deep glad fulness of spiritual life she finds complete satisfaction in the things provided and sanctioned of God, and does not need to mix with God's enemies and rejectors in order to find them. Church members are then saved too high to ask the *low questions* that always betoken a low spiritual life. I never in my life heard any one who was "filled with the Holy Ghost" asking, "Can I do this?" "May I have that?" or, "Will there be any harm in so and so?" when the questions referred to questionable entertainments or amusements. Spirit-filled Christians have left the low levels expressed by

"Is this wrong? that? or the other?" These tastes are dead, and they are possessed of a higher, nobler, more Christlike set of longings. It has become with them, not, "What can I have of the world for myself and still remain saved?" but, "What and how much can I do for Him who has done so much for me?" They see the world in its true light, and by the might of God they put and keep it and its calls, claims, and offers in their proper place.

I am not unchurching people who are church members, but who play cards for money and patronize the theatre, the music hall and the ball-room. No doubt, multitudes of people who indulge in these things have a saving trust in Christ. I have no hard words either for them; but I do want to say just here that I never once knew a man or woman "filled with the Spirit" of God who would go near these amusements. But I have known scores, who loved and patronized these things, drop them at once when they were led to seek and claim a personal pentecost. Aye, and I have known that blessed death to the world and its baubles come to nearly all the members of a church as the result of a real revival.

And, once more, a revival *settles the question of service.* As surely as the heart gets love-filled the hands get work-filled. Service always follows true sonship, and when the love of the son is deep the father's service becomes a joy to him. It was *to save men* that our Lord became a man, went through His earthly ministry, endured His cross and passion, was raised from the dead, commissioned His church, and ascended on high. It was for this He sent the Paraclete, and it is for this above all things that He intercedes and waits. Filled with His love, we are filled with His passionate yearning for the souls of men.

This is the only source of what we call *the passion for souls.* In this the pentecostal church received it, and in this it has come to all who have received it since then. Loving Him fully, we long to give Him constantly His supreme joy, the joy of saving His blood-bought ones. We then also enter into His deep yearning love for our fellow-men, and as the Spirit-filled life is such a blessed life, we long unutterably for others to share it. We cannot then eat our bread of life or drink our living water alone. Ecclesiastical selfishness and laziness alike perish in the Spirit's holy flame. Church members do not then need to be bribed by office, or scolded, or whipped up to do some work for Christ and the unsaved around them. It is their meat and drink, their daily joy to serve the Lord who has saved them.

We are told that, in Roman days, Cato got the idea that it was necessary for Rome's advancement that Carthage should be destroyed. He brooded over the idea till it became a conviction. He warmed the conviction at the fires of his heart until it took possession of his whole being. He got at last to put it into everything he said. When he addressed the Senate, when he greeted a friend, or when he replied to his family, he was sure to add, "But Carthage must be destroyed." It became the absorbing passion of his life.

Aye, and when we are filled with the Spirit of our Lord, and with the word He has given to us, we Christians get *our absorbing passion*, the passion for souls. We enter the secret of our Lord's sore travail for perishing men and His cross; His passion and His loving yearning for the lost becomes ours as never before. The great—though sometimes inarticulate—cry of the soul is, "Whether I am rich or poor, learned or illiterate, smiled upon or frowned upon, famed or unknown, whether my life here is long or brief, by all I can do in life, in word, and deed, *men and women must be saved.*"

The torch of a sacrificial love of man is always lighted at the flame of the love of God. It was in this spirit of love that John Howard lived and died in helping the thousands who were rotting in the prisons of Europe; in this William Lloyd Garrison, Clarkson and Wilberforce, slaved for the freeing of Africa's sons and daughters who were toiling and dying in American chains; in this Livingstone, Hannington, and Mackay lived and died for the swarthy heathen who filled their hearts; and it was this passionate love of men, born of an infilling love of God, that sent the heroic Damien to toil and die

Mr. and Mrs. Waugh.

among his rotting lepers in that far-off South Sea island.

Of this fulness was born the passion for souls that possessed so many of the early Methodist preachers and people, and heroes of Christ in other churches. Through this anointing Whitefield, Wesley, Carey, Brainerd, Stoner and a host of others were what they were in the saving of men. Oh for that old-time passion to possess modern Methodism! What a victorious army our church would be! Oh that all the hosts of God were under this pentecostal might! What days of victory these latter days would be! How a lot of our terrible problems in church and society would be solved in joy and triumph! How the world would feel the power of the Church! How the cold and scornful Haeckels would be sent back among their bottles and crucibles to mind their own business! How the poor dupes of Watts and Blatchford would see the truth, and hurl the little prattlers and their pitiful little nostrums out of the way! How the multitudes in moral serfdom would flock to Jesus for the great deliverance, to find that the sins that had degraded and cursed them could charm and bind them no more!

And this the Lord longs and waits to give to all. It is the privilege and might be the normal life of every Christian to-day. "Be filled with the Spirit" is *our Lord's command* to each of His own, and His command holds our highest good. We have known multitudes of church members who were for years cold, lazy and useless to God and men. Then came a Holy Ghost revival, their spiritual life was revived, and ever since they have been flames of fire in the work of their Lord. May our church, may all the churches, see it! May they all be led to intercession, and to a great spiritual awakening, that through His church our Lord may give us *a national revival!*

CHAPTER XI.

Revivals and the Community.

WE are certainly living in stirring and serious times, and the state of society and the nation is full of profound interest to the thoughtful Christian. Both the bright and the dark sides of the present situation are now so vividly presented to us, as to appeal with irresistible force to all who love their God and their fellow-men. For the brighter and happier lot of the majority of the working classes and of the children of the upper poor and middle classes; for the intense activity of the churches and their more eager diffusion of the knowledge and humane principles of the gospel of Christ; for the assistance rendered to society by the nobler types of socialists; and for the quickened Christian interest and enthusiasm in evangelising the heathen at home and abroad, which nerve our faith and hope,—we are profoundly thankful to God.

But, on the other hand, our social and national blunders are so colossal and costly; our great social and national scourges are so many and powerful, and so terrible in their effects upon their victims; and the problems to which they give birth are so heavy upon the hearts of the church and the nation alike,—that the most careless Christian must feel the burden if he looks and thinks at all.

We are cursed with over-wealth at the top of society, as we are burdened with poverty at the bottom. The unparalleled commercial prosperity of the last few years has made the nation rich as never before. Wealth has led to a pampered luxury of living that is swiftly enervating moral as well as physical fibre, and loosening those spiritual and moral sanctions which have ever been the truest safeguards of society. We are still the most drunken nation on the face of the earth, and the gambling mania is cursing multitudes of men, women, lads and girls in every grade of society. The responsibilities of parenthood are being more than ever shirked by those most equal to them, and prostitution is more than ever a national menace and disgrace. The greed of gold is eating still more deeply into the very fibres of our national character, and the craze for personal pleasure and excitement becomes every year more conscienceless and insane.

As the need for some great change becomes more urgent, the sense of impending change is being more clearly felt. People who think and feel with and for their fellow-men feel sure that important changes of some sort lie in the near future. They feel that the time-spirit is pregnant and are asking what it will bring forth, how it will come, and if we have any personal responsibilities in relation to its coming; and good men and true, though not all taught of God, are trying to answer these questions.

In his splendid little book on "The Next Great Awakening" Dr. Strong has given the best answer I have yet seen, to the above questions. After pointing out that the human constitution and therefore that of society is such, that communities may be expected to make progress through the crises we usually call revivals, he reminds us that we have had four such awakenings in Europe during the last 350 years, and that each one has had its own special message or watchword. Those revivals were, the Reformation, the Puritan Revival, the evangelical revival under Wesley and Whitefield, and the revival that began with the advent to Britain of the late D. L. Moody and Mr. Sankey. He evidently believes that we are on the eve of another great awakening, and tells us that its watchword will be "The Kingdom of God." I heartily endorse nearly every sentence in his splendid little volume.

Soon after its publication, a well-known D.D. gave an address in the West of England to a college of students preparing for the gospel ministry. It may seem presumptuous for an evangelist to criticise a D.D., but I utterly disagree with nearly everything he said, and to glance at a few of the errors of his positions and prophecies may help us towards the truth.

He too believes that an awakening is near, but he assures us that it will come apart from any religious revival. "We had," he says, "a revival of that kind during the missions of Moody and Sankey, but we shall have that sort of thing no more." Since that prophecy was uttered God has given us the 90,000 seekers of the Welsh revival, who are nearly all standing fast to this day! The next revival, he assures us, will not be religious, but "an ethical and social" awakening. Certainly, but these are *fruits* not *roots*, they are *consequences* not *causes*. From what are they to spring? What dynamic will be equal to their production? The watchword of the coming revival is to be "social righteousness and the redemption of our national life." Lovely words these all are, and standing too for glorious realities. We evangelists love those words, and are praying and toiling to bring in the blessed realities they represent.

This wonderful D.D.'s revival is to be apart from "the atonement of Christ" and will not come "through the conversion of the individual." Then, without the light and love of Christ as the soul of it, what will this revival accomplish? What will be its inspiration and sustaining power? The redemption of society will never be accomplished without sacrifice, and the merely "ethical" is seldom *sacrificial.*

There is no altruism like that of the Spirit of Christ and all true "humanism" is born of the love of God.

Society is made up of individuals, and "social righteousness" is *the righteousness of individuals in the mass.* But righteousness of character springs from rightness of heart, and apart from the atonement and Spirit of Christ the human heart is wrong. The wail of Cotter Morrison was that "there is no cure for a bad heart," and that multitudes of men and women around us have got bad hearts. But thank God! if "there is no cure for a bad heart" the Spirit of God can give "a new heart" from which springs righteousness. We cannot have a social and ethical revival that will purify the springs of our social and national life, except as *the result of a spiritual revival.* We cannot have a widespread "social righteousness," apart from a widespread spiritual awakening in which men's hearts are made right by the operation of the Spirit of God.

If "not on the lines of individual conversion," on what lines may we expect this great revival? Our D.D.'s answer is, "We must get away from individualism to collectivism," and that answer is claptrap, a tickle for the ears of the thoughtless socialist. How can we have a redeemed collectivism without redeemed individuals? Of what is the mass composed if not of units? How can we have a regenerated community that is not made up of regenerated men and women? As surely as the individual always goes up heart first, society always goes up individual first.

Our D.D. says, "It has been the custom for a man, when he got converted, to begin at once to praise God for saving him. But if in the next awakening a man is saved, he will withhold his praise to God until he sees what is to become of the unsaved men and women around him." This, my readers, sounds beautifully altruistic, but it is just as hollow and as much a play to the gallery as the previous assertions. For over twenty years men and women have been rescued from social wreckage in connection with my own meetings. Drunkards have become permanently sober, liars truthful, thieves honest, moral lepers pure and clean, and blasphemers have been turned into men of praise and prayer. Brutes have become gentle, coarse men kindly, and fallen lost women have been made pure and good. People over head and ears in debt have been saved, and then have paid up all arrears and incurred such no more.

Multitudes of men and women who were a curse to their families, a disgrace to their friends, and moral plague spots to their communities, are to-day ethically noble, social saviours, and a mighty power in uplifting and blessing the neighbourhoods in which they live. In connection with the Salvation Army, City Missions, and kindred Christian organizations I have myself known thousands of just such rescues achieved in this and in other lands. And I unhesitatingly assert that all such rescues would have been simply impossible to us who have been used of God in achieving them, had we not been ourselves first brought into fellowship with the living Christ for the motives and the power for such work.

If our doctor of divinity had been also a doctor of humanity; if he had not only studied theories, systems, and theologies, but also the sins, sorrows, and needs of the slums; if he had read not only the philosophies of great thinkers, but also the woes of great sinners and sufferers and the triumphs of slum toilers who help to save them; if he had read such stories as "Down in Water Street," and "The Annual Report of the Manchester and Salford Wesleyan Mission," he would have been saved from uttering such ignorant and mischievous nonsense. Apart from the pardon of sin, peace of mind, peace of heart, and rest of conscience a man has in Christ; apart from the deep glad sense of security which pervades and steadies his life; apart from his new promptings and powers for the formation of noblest character; apart from the nerve and cheer put into every step of his life by the Christian's "blessed hope"; apart from all that is purely personal and spiritual; I claim that in the motives, longings and power to help and bless his fellow-men, that come to a man when he is himself converted to God, he has a perfect right there and then to begin "to praise God for saving him." A spiritual awakening is the birthtime and birthplace of an ethical and social awakening, whether in a neighbourhood or in a nation.

With Nunquam's plausible nonsense on this subject I have dealt elsewhere, so only a few words are needed here. His plea is that a social awakening must precede and result in an ethical revival. The want of ethics, he says, is the result of bad economical and social systems and conditions. He acknowledges that a crowd of people are bad, but says "*they* are not to blame," but the conditions that make and keep them bad. He is either too dense to see, or too dishonest to state, that this view really means that all the folly and sin are among the folks at the bottom of society, and his dupes are too dull to see that therefore his views, as Mr. Chesterton and Mr. Haw have so clearly pointed out, are a gross insult to the masses in the slums. *Men* and *women* made the bad "systems and conditions," and are bigger than their works. It is folly to fix the blame upon things *impersonal* like "systems and conditions," and to say that "more perfect conditions would result in more perfect men." Thousands of the worst men in this land are living where the conditions are simply ideal. The way of God, of history and of common sense is, "get the men and women made better and they will help to better the conditions." The ethical life and social conditions of whole neighbourhoods have been bettered and uplifted by the spiritual forces and Christian converts of the revival in Wales. Age after age, in this and other lands, a single saved individual has created a new atmosphere in home, workshop, and neighbourhood, and a real revival has made the district another place to live in. When, through receiving a spiritual dynamic men *go up*, they do something to carry surrounding conditions up with them.

Let us look for instance at the effects of the liquor traffic upon individuals, families, society and the nation, and ask ourselves whether the cure will come from changed legislative or any other conditions, so much as from *changed men.* All must admit that while the drink interest has its present place and power in the land, a deep widespread revival of social righteousness is utterly impossible. If the latter comes, the former must to a very great extent go. Our British drink bill in 1902 meant more than fifty-four pounds for every letter in the whole Bible. It will take Britain more than 100 years, at our present rate of giving, to give as much to Foreign Missions and to the British and Foreign Bible Society as we spent last year *in drink and tobacco alone!* Our drink and tobacco bill last year was more than £200,000,000, and we have never yet as a nation reached £2,000,000 in our giving to the cause of God in foreign lands. And yet we wonder why the nations mock and sneer when we talk about "Christian England," as we ourselves do in this land at the words "*Holy* Russia."

The awful part that drink plays in cursing the people and ruining this nation is known to most, and about the curse and shame of it most of us are agreed. But are we agreed as to the best way out? Socialists like Russell Smart tell us that "poverty is the most fruitful cause of drunkenness." Common sense says that if a man has so little poverty that he can afford to be a drunkard, *he has not enough poverty to drive him to be a drunkard.* Which is right? Where shall we start with the best hope of success? With the conditions, or with the people? All I have seen compels me to say, "Do all you can to change wrong conditions, but do your *first and best to change wrong people.*"

For instance, all are agreed that we have too many drink-shops. Now which is the shortest and best way to reduce their number? I will give my view by means of an illustration. A few years ago I conducted a mission in a country town of perhaps 4,500 inhabitants. Among those laid hold of by the power of God were twelve men who were slaves to drink. By the time we reached the end of the mission, ten of the twelve had been soundly converted to God and the other two were at the farewell service, and both under deep conviction of sin. One of them did not stay to the after-meeting, but the other—whose wife, son and daughter had been saved earlier in the mission—did. When the appeal was made, his daughter, who sat next to him, whispered

"Father, we are now all saved except you, are you going to stay outside?" "No, my lass," he said, "I will settle it now if you will go with me into that inquiry-room." Arm-in-arm the girl and her father went into the room and knelt, and there he found peace through believing. Kissing his daughter in the presence of over sixty inquirers and a fine staff of workers, he said, "This is the angel the Lord sent to lead me the last step to Jesus."

In the meantime, his drinking chum had gone home to his supper. When he got to bed he could not sleep for his sense of sin and need; his conscience loudly told him he should have come out for Christ before leaving the chapel. He got so miserable that he got out of bed and dressed. Having made up the fire he began to pray and cry to God to save him. By five in the morning he was in deepest distress, but feeling very thirsty, he decided to make some tea. While the kettle was boiling he renewed his cries for mercy, and on the stroke of six o'clock he trusted Jesus with his all.

Then his peace and joy were such that he forgot he wanted any tea, and set off to tell his friend that he had got converted. When he entered the street leading to his house, he saw his friend coming to meet him. At once he called out, "Oh, R——! I was just coming to tell you that I have just got saved now at my own fireside." "Why, B——," his friend replied, "I was just coming to tell you that I got saved at chapel last night." Then the dear fellows joined hands there, and sang over and over again, amid tears of joy, "Praise God, from whom all blessings flow!" As they sang, windows were thrown up, heads came out, and as the situation was understood, tears of glad sympathy were soon dropping into many a front garden and upon many a doorstep.

Now, note the sequel. Two years after this the Wesleyans there had a second spiritual birthday tea-meeting, specially for the converts of that mission. The meeting deputed an official to come and see me at Barnsley, to report progress and to bring me prayers and greetings. I was then in mission in Barnsley, and he gave, among other cheering results, the above facts to my crowded audience, and closed by saying, "That man B—— died a few months ago, a happy triumphant death, and *the other eleven* reclaimed drunkards *were all in my class-meeting last week.* God has kept the whole twelve steadfast on the rock." Who will close the drink-shops we do not need? *The brewers and distillers.* When? *When men and women stop going to them to drink.* When will that be? *When they have got soundly converted.* When people drink freely of God's "living water" that blesses, they do not want man's damning concoctions that destroy. Thus a revival is the first and shortest road to a reduction in the number of drink-shops in the land.

As a wider illustration, the revival in Wales is

a fine object lesson in the connection between an evangelical and an ethical revival. I am told by unbiassed observers that the results of the revival upon society are as beautiful as they are unanswerable. In the revival area the takings of the drink-shops have run down gloriously, in many cases as much as six-sevenths. The money once wasted on drink is now spent on food, clothing, furniture, pictures, ornaments, and the hundred and one things that nourish trade and minister to the real needs and comfort of the people. Books too, *especially Bibles*, are being bought as never before, and the tradesmen on every side are rejoicing. People who were in debt have paid what they owed, in many cases debts owing for fourteen or fifteen years.

The magistrates in the revival districts have had more "maiden sessions" and more "white gloves" during the last twelve months than in the preceding five years. As "the fear of the Lord is the beginning of wisdom" the men converted are no longer fools enough to put their money into the hands of book-makers, and those gentry have had to go and find their flats and greenhorns elsewhere. Blasphemy has almost ceased among the men, and the "Diolch Iddo" has taken its place. Unionists and non-unionists, who in pit or quarry used to meet with scowls of hate, now meet with "God bless you!" and often have a word of prayer before they begin their toil. Family feuds and religious intolerance have been burnt up in the holy flame, and hearts, homes and churches are one in the bonds of love.

If these results are not "ethical," what are they? If these are not in the line of "a redeemed national life," if they do not spell "social righteousness," then in the name of common sense what do such words mean?

A few months ago, the editor of "The Clarion" gave great amusement to people who think, and great encouragement to his little atheists who have little with which to think, by trying to answer the above questions. Some one had evidently told the little man about Charles Darwin, and about his theory of "reversion to type." Though a baby at facts Mr. Blatchford is a giant with words, and this word seems to have stuck in his memory, and he uses it to explain the phenomena of the Welsh revival.

He tells us that the area of the movement is studded with churches, chapels, sabbath-schools, mission rooms and kindred Christian institutions. That texts from the Bible, verses from Christian hymns, sentences and sentiments from them and from the lips of Christian teachers and professors, and the influences connected with them, have surrounded and been drilled into the inhabitants all their lives. That these sentences, sentiments, verses and influences have lain dormant in these people's hearts for years, and now a wave of feeling and excitement has passed over the district, moving these men and women and waking these slumbering messages and influences into activity, and producing these remarkable results. They have *reverted* to early teachings and impressions, and have not been *converted* at all.

Well, my readers, I am so profoundly impressed by Nunquam's nonsense that I venture to make a solemn promise. If any man will show me that Haeckel, Blatchford and other infidel teachers are putting into the memories, minds and hearts of the young people and others who are under their influence, such passages and hymn-verses, I care not from what books; such impressions and influences, I care not from what people; that if touched by some passing excitement or emotion in the future, they will work out into such results as we see to-day in the wake of the Welsh revival, I will turn over a new leaf in my attitude towards infidelity. I have been hitting it all through my ministry, and during the last two years have given more "Christian evidence" and "anti-infidel" sermons and lectures than in all my life before. But show me that infidel teachers are sowing for such a future ethical harvest as this in Wales among Britons and the one in Fiji among the heathen, and I will henceforth bless the infidel and oppose him no more.

No, the wrong in conditions, systems and societies springs from the wrong in the hearts of men. "Man's inhumanity to man" is the starting point of the mischief and the injustice, and his bad heart is the source of it. Only Christ can put that right, and as men are righted systems and surroundings will be righted too. Evangelism is *humanism*, and the saving of men is the best kind of *patriotism*. The noblest altruism is the sacrifice of self in the saving of those around us. If social conditions are to be permanently bettered, if the power of our great national sins is to be shattered and this sin and sorrow-cursed land of ours be turned into a noble happy England, we must sacrifice toil and pray for a nation-wide spiritual revival.

CHAPTER XII.

The Value of Permanence.

As the great end to be kept in view in all Christian service, the permanence of results can hardly be exaggerated. It means *nearly everything*, for if that is not secured the sacrifice, prayer, and toil of the workers have been largely in vain. In my "Special Missions" I have replied fully to the oft-repeated, but utterly unworthy and untruthful assertion, that the effects of special services are evanescent and the converts nearly all fall away. It is therefore unnecessary to write more than a few words about it here. That statement is usually uttered in the form of a sneer, and is usually an attempt to justify personal laziness, personal indifference to or personal failure in, the work of saving men. I never met a man much used of God in saving others, who was foolish and unchristian enough thus to disparage all round the results of special services.

Personally, though the sneer never hurts me, I do all that lies in my power to make its utterance an impossibility to a truthful man. I can hardly conceive of any greater calamity coming to a church, than to have a lot of people join it who are *not converted*. If in any series of meetings they have been emotionally stirred and excited, both they and the church may mistake the mere human emotion for a work of grace. But if the sinfulness of sin has not been realised, if there has been no deep sense of a personal need of a personal Saviour, if there has been no surrender of the will and the affections to Christ, and no new life imparted to them by the Spirit of God, then they are *not saved*. If the church does not realise this and succeed in leading them from the surface feeling to the deeper sense of need and then to Him who alone can supply that need, then it is a catastrophe for these people to become church members.

In most cases of this kind the usual results are simply heart-breaking to all who have helped to bring them in and disastrous to the work of God as a whole. If "the root of the matter" is not in these new members, there is nothing left but disappointment when the excitement is gone. When the gush and glow of their emotional stir has subsided, they have nothing left as a compensation for the worldly pleasures and companionships they gave up when they thought they were converted. Not made "partakers of the Divine nature," they have nothing in common with spiritually-minded people, and are more fully in touch with their old companions and friends. The things of God have no more charm for them than have the people of God, and they gradually forsake the means of grace and slip back into the old life and ways. Not being saved themselves, they have no passion for the saving of others, and hence Christian work has no attraction for them, and hence, in their spare time, their heads, hearts and hands must be filled elsewhere than in a Christian church.

All this is full of pain to the toilers in the church, who have prayed and laboured for months or years. They did all they could to bring these people to the meetings and to Christ. They rejoiced over them with a great joy when they thought they had decided to be the Lord's. They lovingly watched over them, and sought to lead them deeper and higher into the life and service of Christ. And when such objects of intercession, sacrifice, toil, tears and rejoicing go back into the world, the pain and disappointment are terrible. Unless they lean hard on God and feel sure that they have done their best to nurse and teach them, the collapse strikes both at their zeal and their faith, and tends to paralyse their efforts for the saving of others.

Then there are others of these unsaved new members of the church who do not leave it. They stay on with their names on the books, and have a name to live while they are dead. When strong temptation meets them, having no Divine power with which to resist it, they fall and bring discredit on the church and give "occasion for the enemies of God to blaspheme." Nearly all the ghastly moral delinquencies that thus work such terrible mischief in and against the churches are among unsaved church members. Here again we see what a tragedy it is to get people into a church who are not "in Christ." And all this is in addition to the awful spiritual peril of people who think they were saved when they were only excited, and who rest upon that experience to the end of their lives. The longer I watch these things, the more completely I feel that *ingatherings* that do not result in *increases* are among the worst things that can come to a church.

Unless those for whom we pray and toil are *converted*, the great end is not reached. That is the end of the church's intercession for the unsaved, of the preacher's evangel to them, and of the work in the sabbath-school. So far as the unsaved are concerned, their conversion is the end of our church, chapel and mission hall building, and of all our church intercession, care and toil. Until made anew, they are of no use either in or for the church. The pastor cannot teach dead men, the church cannot nurse and feed unborn babes, those who are not Christ's saved ones themselves cannot be Christ's saviours of others. "Ye *must* be born from above," is our Lord's word to all who would be His, and the new birth is the only door into the new life.

Holding such strong views as to the value of permanence, I do all that I can personally and through my workers to avoid mere human results. A mere *man's mission* is worse than no mission at all, for only Divine results are lasting and blessed. Of course, in a large work of God, when scores each night are entering the inquiry-rooms, there are almost sure to be some who enter them without any counting of the cost and without any real repentance. Caught in the contagion of feeling or example, they may make a public confession of Christ and be quite sincere though quite mistaken.

When people come out in such numbers, the inquiry-room often becomes a difficulty as well as the deep and legitimate feeling in the meetings. It is indeed no easy thing to find in one meeting from seventy to a hundred experienced Christians who can sit down by the side of penitent sinners and intelligently point them to Christ. The difficulty is all the greater if the inquirers are not quite sick of a Christless life, and not clear as to why they are there. One thing I here mention with great thankfulness and without conceit. In nearly every mission I conduct, the inquiry-room workers tell me how easy and delightful they find their work to be. The great reason for this, as I have pointed out in a previous chapter, is that I do all I can to make the inquiry-room work as easy as possible by making the pulpit and pew work as deep and clear as possible.

But, even then, the work in the inquiry-room is not always patient and clear, and when large numbers want help there, many of them get very little of personal counsel and prayer. The result is that some fall away, and in very large missions, in neighbourhoods where the people are more emotional than ethical, sometimes a large number fall away. But blessed be God! larger numbers still stand fast, and become witnesses and workers for their new Lord and Master.

And what would one expect but that *some* would lapse, under such conditions? All candidates are not accepted, all competitors do not pass, and all the children born do not survive. In some churches, true converts have but little chance. I was shown round a church the other day by one of the officials, and he informed me that it was too true that for long years they had had *everything except religion.* Real converts are often connected with other churches than the one in which they have been led to Christ. In those churches there may be very few who have any real sympathy with either missions or their converts, and the spiritual babes sent there have a poor prospect of being nursed and fed. You cannot hatch chickens among icicles, and a lot of churches are more like refrigerators than incubators. Through getting into such places, young converts are often discouraged and starved out, and then dubbed "backsliders."

But this is more or less true of all forms of saving work, and is not confined to special missions.

In a real revival, the church is blessed with a quickened spiritual life. If an inquirer be soundly converted and joins such a church, he is more likely to be well cared for and helped along the way than if he joined an unrevived church at an ordinary time. When a church has travailed sorely and sacrificed and worked hard for souls, she is the most likely and the most fit to care for and treasure them when won. This is fully confirmed by facts all round. The saddest backslidings are often those of old unsaved church members who have reached middle life, and not among young folks and the converts of missions. The most pitiful and disastrous lapses I have ever known have been among those in "the midst of the years," and in churches where there has been no revival for years.

Nevertheless, whether in mission, in a return visit, or in the open air, in all my work at all times, I make permanence the chief end of all I do, and I earnestly urge it upon all who are engaged in Christian toil. I never forget a lesson I got from a word of John Wesley's, that I read when I entered this work. He was revisiting, on horseback, a town in the Black Country where he had toiled some six months previously. He was joined on the road by a man who knew him, but who had no sympathy with him or with his work. Presently they came to where a drunken man was lying on the side of the road. "Do you see that drunken man, Mr. Wesley?" said his fellow-traveller. "Certainly," replied Wesley. "Well," said the man, "he is one of *your converts*." "Very likely," replied Wesley; "if he had been one of the Lord's converts He would have made a better job of him."

A beautiful answer, and wise too! There is nothing I dread so much in a mission as *man's converts*. They are worse than none at all, and my great aim is to have as few of them as possible in my missions. And upon this constant effort to let the work be Divine and therefore lasting, God has set unmistakeable seals of approval. A few of these I now wish to mention, not for any self-glorification, but for the encouragement of all who are engaged in saving work, and especially of those whose work is among what is called "unpromising material."

A few years ago, with the assistance of friends in different parts of the country, I sought to get an approximate idea of the number of my sons in the gospel who were themselves then preachers of that gospel. Since then, I have tried to keep note of the increasing numbers as I have come across or heard of them. As nearly as I can tell, there are now nearly nine hundred of my sons in Christ *whom we know to be preachers of the gospel* in this and in other lands. They are clergymen, curates and Nonconformist ministers, scores of them are in our own ministry at home and abroad, hundreds of them are local preachers, and many of them are officers in the Salvation Army. If it be my Lord's will, I hope to live and toil until I know of a thousand of my sons preaching the gospel that saved both them and me.

In the last chapter I gave the striking case of twelve drunkards who were all kept standing steadfast for two years, and who, for anything I have heard to the contrary, are being kept still. In the chapter on "The Joy of Service," in my "Sonship and Service," I have given three glad illustrations of God's keeping power, that I only need mention here. One is of a journey from Ipswich to Penzance on which, at five different points, I met with converts of past missions, and heard from them of others who were doing well, several of them having become preachers of the gospel. Another was of the meeting on an Atlantic liner of five of my local-preacher converts, all *en route* for Manitoba. The third was of a naval officer converted when I was in Cork, and who six years later brought me greetings from his six friends converted the same night, kneeling by his side, now all of them workers for Christ. To these I may be permitted to add a few more cases that have greatly cheered my heart in the work I love so well.

When I went some four years ago for my second mission in A——, I found that the circuit steward, the teacher of the men's Bible class, and nine more of my best helpers were the fruit of my first mission there some twelve years before. In my last mission at B—— the minister told me that he had discovered that a large proportion of my splendid staff of helpers were the converts of my mission held in the same chapel thirteen years previously. One of the grandest missions I ever had was in one of our largest chapels, and the work went on until six hundred people joined the churches of the town and circuit. It is now six years since that mission was held, and up to now I have only been able to hear of two of the converts who have lapsed. Kindred cases might be given all over the land; and if any of my readers are sceptical, they can have names both of places and individuals.

Turning from places to individuals may help to encourage and strengthen our faith in the keeping power of God and the self-perpetuating character of Christian work. I pray daily for all my colleagues, and rejoice eagerly in the blessing that rests upon their labours. But, while they are all in my brotherly love and earnest prayers, it is only natural that my deepest interest is in John Grange Bennett. It is now nearly twenty years since, at the close of one of my addresses, he bowed in the pew and handed over his life to Christ. From that time until now he has been winning men to his Lord, and I rejoice over his work with pleasure and grateful joy. Already he has converts in the ministry, and quite a string of them are local preachers. Some of my best helpers, where I have crossed his path, have been his spiritual children. Only a few months ago a gray-haired man made the smiles and tears come to many eyes as he seized my hand in a chapel and said: "I am older than you, Mr. Waugh, but you are my grandfather." When I asked him how that came to be, he said, "Well, you are Grange Bennett's spiritual father, and he is mine."

One of my grandest off-Sundays was at Eastbrook, Bradford, last April, and the harvest of men at night was glorious. I have very seldom risen to address an audience with the tears in my eyes, but I did that afternoon. The hall was packed with the men's "Brotherhood" till many had to stand. Their pastor, that grand lad Herbert Nield, was in the chair. When he told them how, more than seventeen years before, I had led him to Christ at Widnes, and that his heart's prayer was that I might do the same for them that day, there were many more wet faces present than the evangelist's. Two years and a half ago I had a letter from one of our superintendent ministers in South Africa. It was to inform me that he had just discovered that his two colleagues, like himself, were my sons in the gospel.

Years ago, in one of my Lancashire missions, one of the most notorious sinners in the town was converted. He was a poacher, a pugilist and a drunkard, he was dressed in rags, and his home was a hell of misery. Though his wife was saved some two and a half years later, everything at home then was dead against him in his new life. That man is now, and has been for years, conducting missions among his fallen fellow-men, and has led hundreds of them to his own saving, keeping, Lord.

During the last few years I have again and again had young men and young women seeking Christ in my meetings, whose parents were saved under my earlier ministry of the word. A large number of my sons in the gospel have been my chairmen for my lectures, and a short time ago I had two such on successive days. For years now quite a number of my happiest homes have been with my own spiritual children. And what a joy it is to be entertained in a home where an host or hostess, and sometimes both, are the converts of some previous visit!

"Mission converts nearly all fall away!" Bless the Lord, no! A few may, as a few of one-by-one converts do, but the vast proportion of them stand fast in the Lord. I could fill chapter after chapter with such known facts and proofs, but they are not needed where there is no prejudice. The cases I have given I could not have given, had they been testimonies to any merit or gift in myself; but they are testimonies to the keeping grace of God, and to Him we ascribe all the glory of them. We preach not a dead but a living Christ, and because He "ever liveth to make intercession for us" He is as able to keep as He is to save, and as willing to use as He is to keep.

CHAPTER XIII.

The Value of Church Membership.

I SINCERELY thank God for the wonderful saving work accomplished during the first visit to this country of the late Mr. Moody and Mr. Sankey. I am grateful for the wonderful impetus and evangelical tone that movement gave to aggressive Christian work nearly all over the kingdom, and for the very definite emphasis given to that movement by the work of the Salvation Army. To that work the church of God in this land owes more to-day than any one can express.

But most privileges can be abused, and most messages can be distorted by perverted human nature. And one of the most pitiful outcomes of the glorious Moody and Sankey and Salvation Army revival has been the sanction drawn from it for a lot of irresponsible free-lance evangelism, that has led to *a widespread and disastrous depreciation of the value and importance of church membership*. A part of the responsibility for this rests upon the churches, that preferred a decorous dulness to warmth and life, and gave no sympathy or encouragement to aggressive effort or to the earnest few among them who loved and longed for it. I believe that between 1875 and 1895 not less than 100,000 people left the ranks of Methodism for the Salvation Army and for undenominational missions. Multitudes of these people, I admit, were not a great loss to us, but thousands of them were good earnest souls that we could ill afford to do without.

But an equal responsibility lies with many of those who have thus left the churches and are leaving them to-day. Because their church had little saving fervour they made it less, by withdrawing their own; because the church was cold they forsook it, instead of trying to warm it; because it was asleep they left it, instead of trying to awaken and rouse it. They did not realize that there were other hearts there as hungry for souls as their own, and longing to see the church saved into a passion for saving the lost. They did not stop to find these church members and form with them a band of intercession for the church and the people. Too often they acted as if the church was dead and past praying for. They assumed that the "cash-nexus" and pride of numbers were the only reasons why the church wanted them as members, and so they went out from among us. Thousands of them are now dead, thousands of them are yet doing splendid work for God and men, thousands of them have learnt their lesson and in the last few years have come back into the churches; but thousands of them have gone back into the world and sin.

I have already in this volume expressed my admiration of and thankfulness for our great central denominational and undenominational missions, yet many of the best of such missions have their special dangers in relation to church membership, because of their greater attractions. The distinctly evangelical preacher, nearly always there; the special choir or string or brass band; the shorter, brighter service; the warmer, easier, and more stirring or more emotional hymns; the fuller part taken by the hearers in the service; free seats, and the absence of exclusive pew doors; and the greater facilities for enjoying it all without the usual responsibilities and cost of church membership,—all count for a great deal. The very *cheapness* of the gospel for mission-room hearers is a grave peril to many of them, for we cannot without spiritual loss take, for a trifle once a week, a gospel we can afford and ought to generously support and spread. It distorts the vision and withers the heart to shirk the financial sacrifice we ought to make in church life and work. The worshipper is almost lost, who looks upon such financial support as "paying for the water of life." It is only paying to get the pipes laid down, and they will not get the water without the pipes. It is a common saying with Brother Witheredheart and Sister Mean-soul that "in the regular churches they are always after money." So far as *their* "money" is concerned, the churches must be *very slow*, for they have not overtaken it yet. Such people never seem to ask where the money comes from that helps to carry on these missions and to make finances easy to the hearers. If they will read the yearly appeals made on behalf of these missions, and study the subscription lists and the platforms at the anniversaries, it may dawn upon them that the great bulk of it comes from members of the "regular churches" of which they speak.

Of course, I do not for a moment blame either the missioners in charge of these places, or those on their staff, for these sad results. These form part of the results of the abuse of a grand privilege, by mean or foolish people. The case is still worse in a multitude of smaller missions that are but the ecclesiastical resort of the self-willed who in no church can have all their own sweet way; of those who *will be* leaders, though without the necessary gifts and graces; and of those who think they can save people by much sound without sense. Short-lived and mischievous are many of these Jack's-as-good-as-his-master-shops, and too often their end is the loss of little souls that with care and patience might have been saved to the end.

In many quarters, it is in these days the popular thing for Christians to be proud of what can only be to them a source of loss. They half boast that while "members of *the church*, they are not connected with any church; that they go here and there, anywhere and everywhere." That is, they are ecclesiastical tramps; and I never knew either God or men get much good out of those whose religion is mostly in their feet. Given a revival, a convention, or any great religious stir—and these dear souls are there, especially if they are not likely to be called upon for much cash or sacrifice. They are never at home except when away from it. They cannot breathe except in a gale. They are never settled except when excited. They are never at rest except in a storm. They think they are broad when they are only shallow. They mistake their lack of creed and conviction for tolerance and broad sympathies. They spread their little power and influence over such a wide area, that there is no weight that counts in any one place. Bless these dear little mistaken souls! Don't some of us know them? We know them so well that we can spot them at once in a meeting, and we could almost pick them out if the lights went out.

I have already admitted, and again assert, that I believe salvation to be possible outside all the churches, and that people are saved in connection with agencies that are outside regular church organisation and membership. We are often told by broad and charitable people that "there are multitudes of saved people outside all the churches." I do not reach that all-round symmetry of Christian character and that effectiveness of Christian service to which we are all called in Christ Jesus.

The churches hold most of the church, and the church is the channel and repository of Christian truth. A child of God will get needed light and teaching there that he cannot get outside. The Holy Spirit, as her light and life, indwells the church, and through her dispenses Divine grace and truth. The church is one by the bond of love, and, even in the poorest specimens of churches, she loves her own better than the world; and the individual Christian will get help and sympathy there that he cannot get elsewhere. The coal that burns hot, among the rest in the fire, turns cold when laid alone, and the fires of devotion to the living Lord and of passion for perishing men are kindled by the Holy Spirit who indwells the body of Christ upon earth. Organised warfare too is nearly always more effective than guerilla warfare, and in church fellowship most Christians can do more and better service for their Lord's cause than if they stand and work alone. And is not this after all the real "schism" of the New Testament? It is the refusal of one member of the body to co-operate with the other members in carrying out the will of the Head, which is Christ.

When I urge these considerations upon godly men who are not in church fellowship, they often plead that they are experienced Christians and can stand fast in the truth, and conquer self, the world, and the devil, without the help and sympathy of church membership, and also do some work for the Lord whom they know and love. But, even if this were fully true, they are not in the first and truest place as witnesses for Christ, and their witness therefore has not its true influence over the world. They may think this to be true when it is not, because they may be unconscious of their loss. And again, if they can successfully conquer and toil alone, what about their families? and what of weak and young Christians who are near them and under their influence? These may not have years of long experience of Christian teaching and experience behind them, and to such, "the communion of saints" may be an *absolute necessity*. So those who think they "can live and work as well for Christ outside such fellowship as inside" may become a very perilous example indeed, and lead some, who follow them, to fall where they themselves can stand. The fact is that no saved person can afford, for their own sake, for the sake of others, or for the Lord's sake, to stay outside fellowship with some section of the visible church of God.

Holding such deep convictions on this matter, I of course always urge all the converts in my missions to get connected at once with some body of believers in Christ. I can never be thankful enough for all the help and blessing I received from taking the same course at my own conversion. As already stated, I land? Again and again men and women have told me in grateful joy how in sorrow they were comforted, in distress relieved, in difficulty supported and helped, and, when almost in despair, lifted up to hope and victory by the members of the churches to which they belonged.

My feelings on the importance of this matter are so strong that, in most cases, I prefer the narrower sphere of evangelistic opportunity in a church to the wider one in an undenominational hall or tent. In saying this, I am not in the least degree reflecting upon the magnificent work done in these places by men like Gipsy Smith, John McNeill and George Clarke. I admire, love, and thank God for these men, and pray for them daily as I do for my own colleagues. I often, under the auspices of the Free Church Council, conduct such missions myself. People will come into such places who will not enter a Methodist chapel, so that we reach material under those circumstances, that we cannot reach elsewhere.

Nevertheless I am not so satisfied with the *final results*, though at the time the numerical results are usually larger. There is *a spiritual-home feeling* about a church that you do not have in hall or tent, and that becomes a kind of *church-bond* to most church converts. The child born in gipsy tent or caravan, or that of the poor vagrant, born by the way-side, cannot have the wise and tender care and nursing given to those who are born into a loving home. Even those born in the modern workhouse miss the loving solicitude and sympathetic watchfulness of the good home, that mean so much to a child's chance of life.

Given a large mission in a hall, and a number of churches taking part in it, no one particular church feels *specially responsible* for the nursing, teaching, training and general care of the converts. At the close of the mission the birth-place of the babes in Christ has to be abandoned, and *the newly born are often the least equal to removals.* But, if led to Christ in a denominational place of worship, the church there feels specially responsible for their oversight and helping on the way; and the place is made familiar to the converts during the mission, if not by their previously belonging to the congregation, and a kind of glad and sacred tie is established between it and them. More than that, there are, on their own church premises, ways of approach to the hearts and consciences of the unsaved seatholders and members of the sabbath-school, that you cannot have elsewhere. And while in the town hall or public hall we may get a wide circle of non-church-goers, and the unsaved from other congregations, we are not so likely to get a large proportion of those we most want, because they become, as a rule, the most useful.

And, after all, those "lost in the house," the unsaved sons and daughters of people in the church, and the regular unsaved hearers, present to us *the finest possible harvest-field.* The thief, the drunkard, and the Magdalene need us and our gospel, and have a great claim upon us. They need the Saviour almost more than any others, and our hearts are glad when we lead them to Him. But what will-less weaklings they have mostly made themselves! What ties bind them to past sins! What an environment they have formed round themselves! And what watching and care they need, for all the rest of their lives! And how little many of them can ever do for the saving of others!

But save the unsaved, already in church and sabbath-school, and you have seldom any such difficulties. Their life-powers and influence are then to be used henceforth for Christ. Born in the church, they join the church, and having its loving sympathy, guidance and care, they become an active and powerful part of it, and add to the power of its witness for the Lord "till He come." Because I set such a high price upon church membership, I prize results like these above all the other results with which the Lord crowns my toil.

Chapter XIV.

Work and Workers.

Two of the most important lessons drilled into me, during my long and wide experience, are *the necessity for every Christian to be a Christian worker*, and *the necessity for getting born leaders into leading places in the work.* Let us take the two thoughts in order.

The terms "Christian" and "Christian worker" ought to be synonymous, for the Christian who is not a Christian worker is an anomaly. The man or woman who claims to be saved, but does no saving, is untrue to one of the first and greatest purposes of God in leading them to Christ. It is as true spiritually as it is physically, that a child cannot be born of only one parent. I write it reverently, and with a hushed spirit, but I believe that while God is *the Father* the church is *the mother* of all "the children of God." We are not only "born of God" but born of His church, who has been "in travail" until she has "brought forth" children.

Few Christians stand in such peril as those who "are at ease in Zion," and few sins are so severely denounced in the word of God as *the sin of laziness.* What a string of dark and deadly sins have been denounced in sermons preached from the words, "Be sure your sin will find you out!" and yet, the one sin about which this warning was uttered was that of laziness. It was for not "coming to the help of the Lord" that His curse fell upon Meroz. The New Testament is equally strong, for "to him that knoweth to do good and doeth it not *to him it is sin.*" The "goats" at our Lord's left hand are to be doomed because of *not doing* good, and the vine-branch to be thrown to the fire is the one that "beareth not fruit." Nor can we wonder at this, for what can be more cruel and selfish than for a saved man to shirk saving work? It is therefore one of the most fruitful causes of backsliding, especially among well-to-do Christians in middle life.

Whatever else we may or may not have, "this salvation" is the "one thing needful" and the greatest good that can come to us between our cradle and our coffin. It hallows our friendships, it purifies our joys, it sweetens our sorrows, it lightens our burdens, and its eternal hope nerves and cheers us in every step of the journey of life. If we have money we must leave it; if we have health it will leave us; if we have dear friends we must say to them the last good-bye. Whatever earthly good we may have or acquire, it is short-lived; but our life in Christ is eternal, and all of the Christ-character and Christ-service into which it brings us, we shall have for ever. The greatest day of our past was the day when we became Christ's, and being His is the greatest of all the blessings we can ever have.

This being so, it is just the greatest blessing to which we can help our fellow-men; and if we refuse, then our sin, and therefore our peril and loss, are great indeed. Is our own sin all forgiven? Are the fetters of evil habit broken and taken away from us? Is the stain of past sin washed out? Are our evil desires uprooted? are heaven-born desires filling our hearts in their place? Does the Spirit of God indwell us, to comfort, to guide, to empower, to use, and to make us more meet for the Homeland day by day? Have we rest of mind, rest of heart, and peace of conscience in Christ day by day? Is our surrendered and trusting life pervaded by a deep glad sense of security that nothing of earth can touch? When we look forward, have we "hope in our death" that it will end in "the resurrection of life"? Is there a "second death" that we shall miss because we have had a second birth? Is there a future of blessedness that will be ours for ever with the Lord whom we love and with our saved dear ones?

Are these things so? If saved, we profess and say they are so, in conversation, sermon, prayer and song? Is it true? Are we honest? If so, do these things meet our highest, deepest need, and constitute our deepest, highest good? You say "Yes!" Then if this new life be this to us, it must be the very best thing and the most needed thing for those around us. This follows the other most surely, and with these lost ones in His mind and word, God says to all His saved ones, "*Go ye* . . . to every creature." To do something we all have some power and opportunity. It is not enough to try to cover cowardice and laziness under the plea, "I live the life." *We are all to do that, and to work as well.* The grace of God has come to us for *work* as well as for *life*, we are called to service as well as to holiness. If we cannot preach or even teach, we can pray for those who do, we can speak to that one, write to the other one, and invite the next one to come under the Spirit and word of God. If we refuse to work, we are guilty of flagrant disobedience to God, and are thwarting one of His great purposes in saving us.

Then think of such treatment of the unsaved! We claim to have received the most blessed deliverance from the most awful peril, yet do nothing to rescue those yet in danger. We say we have found the best and dearest Friend that man or woman may know, yet do nothing to lead others into His friendship. We claim to be day by day nearing a future, of the glory and blessedness of which "the half has never been told," yet never earnestly plead with others to go with us. When the four lepers in the Syrian camp realized that, in self-seeking amid the plenty around them, they had forgotten the starving city,

Mr. and Mrs. Waugh's Eldest Son
(The late Stanley T. Waugh).

they were conscience-stricken, and said, "We do not well, this day is a day of good tidings, and we hold our peace." If their *silence* was *sinful*, what must ours be if we do not tell the perishing around us of Him who is "the bread of life" indeed?

The most perplexing person I ever meet is the man or woman who claims to be saved and to believe the Bible, and yet does nothing to save others. And yet, how hard it is to get such people to see how in this abstention from Christian work they are disobeying God and cruelly wronging their fellow-men! How people arrange their views to ease their consciences, until they cannot see the truth! For instance, there are crowds of professing Christians who would think they had committed a terrible sin if they went to a dance or a theatre or took a glass of whisky, who have apparently no idea that in cherishing an unforgiving spirit they are sinning far more deeply against their own souls. There are people who never dream that through a constant display of a selfish bad temper they are doing more to wreck a home and send the young folks in it to the world and the devil, than they would by going to theatre five nights a week and having a whisky toddy when they got back. And harder still is it to get men and women to see how terribly they sin against God and men, by abstention from Christian work, though many of them would shrink aghast from things not half so sinful in the sight of God.

For nearly thirty years I have been thanking God that I was set to work for Him as soon as I was led to Him. In urging the converts in my meetings to get to work at once, I always tell them that I have never had time to be a backslider. Beginning to work for Christ at my conversion I have been kept at it ever since, to my own help and blessing as well as that of others. I remember that in my newly-found joy I asked the Lord to make and keep me the kind of Christian the devil does not like, and I have ever since tried to live up to that prayer. What has been such a joy and help to me, I always urge upon all who are entering the Christian life.

What can God do for a lazy Christian, who is disloyal to His purposes and the needs of the perishing? While thus treating God and men there can be no deep personal spiritual life or growth in the grace and knowledge of Jesus Christ. Such people often say to me, "Each time you come to us you seem to be mightily enjoying the religion you preach to us." "Yes," I reply, "I *do* enjoy my religion, twenty-four hours per day and three hundred and sixty-five days per year." "Well," they say, "I am often so cold and dead that I hardly know whether or not I have any religion at all." When I ask them if they do any work for Christ and the saving and blessing of men, they usually answer me with a long-drawn-out, "Well, no." "Then," I always say, "you deserve to starve."

You have seen a man digging in a garden on a

keen, cold, spring morning. In a few minutes he straightens up, takes his handkerchief and wipes the perspiration off his face, and says to the neighbour who is idly looking on, "My word, but it is getting warm! We shall have the summer upon us directly." A few minutes later, and the neighbour buttons his jacket and says, "My word, but it is cold! There is not much sign of the summer yet, my friend." The men are both in the same temperature, but the one is warm because he is working and the other is cold because he is doing nothing. It is the same in the church of God. Nearly all the cheeriest, brightest, most confident and content Christians, are those who are working hard for the blessing of others. Giving, they receive and blessing, they are blest. It is as true spiritually as in temporal things, "There is that giveth and yet increaseth, and there is that withholdeth and it tendeth to poverty."

All those who read these lines, and who are newly converted, I again urge not only to join some church *at once*, but to get into some kind of Christian work *at once.* You will have less time to talk and argue with the devil, and to think of the things you have left for Christ's sake. Your work will send you to the study of God's word and of other helpful books, and thus bless your own soul as well as keep you out of the way of many temptations. Work is a fine thing for keeping us out of a mischief. A horse cannot be *kicking* while it is *pulling*, and nearly all church of the chapel where I was toiling was a gang of thirty young men, whose leader was a big powerful fellow called Jack. They were up to and ready for anything in the shape of mischief, and some of their exploits I dare not put on paper. In the district they were called "the rebels," and their leader "the Mahdi." The meetings attracted the whole gang, Jack and his wife got converted, and before the mission closed *the whole thirty turned to Christ.* The minister and officials were wise enough to form them into a mission band, and to allow Jack, assisted by another man, to remain their leader. They went to the adjoining village and started cottage services. Their success was such that the owner of the cottage knocked that and the adjoining cottage into one. Even then the folks who had got saved and those who wanted to get saved could not all get in. The brave fellows set to work to toil and beg, and with a bit of financial assistance soon had up a useful chapel which for years has been the birthplace of souls for God. The sins and wild life of his early manhood have cost Jack a heavy price in health since then, but there he is still, a fine witness to the saving power of God.

In a men's meeting I conducted years ago, in a town in the Midlands, the last man to come forward seeking Jesus was a powerful young fellow, with a wide influence and connected with his father's large business. How he wept over the wild sinful years just behind him, and over his sad influence over the two hundred men they employed! What an agony of repentance his was to be sure! I never witnessed more poignant conviction or more bitter sorrow in a penitent in my life. I had been told a great deal about him and the sad influence of his godless life, and there could be no mistake about his force of character. My host, one of the ministers, and I entered into a compact of prayer for him, specially as being the key to an important position. On that second Sunday afternoon of the mission our prayers were gloriously answered.

Nearly everybody in the district knew the man, and his conversion made a profound sensation. That very night his unmarried sister was saved, and his only brother the following night. On the Tuesday one of his workmen had a sad accident, and while he lay unconscious his young master was sent for. When the poor fellow opened his eyes he thought he was dying, and looking up into the face of the man saved two days before, he said, "Gaffer, pray with me." Down went the dear fellow on his knees among those rough working men and prayed for the stricken man by his side, and more men were saved that week through his decision and brave stand than we shall ever know in this world; but over eight hundred decided for God in the two weeks of the mission.

At once the man got into harness and is in it still, a leader of men for God. In my next mission in that chapel that gentleman was my host and helper.

London I saw that the Sunday-school was the one element of hope about the place. I saw too, as did also the pastor and his wife, that a young woman of twenty was the commanding personality of the whole school and therefore the key to the position. Pleading the promise in Matthew xviii. 19, we united in prayer for her conversion and before the first week closed she made a public confession of Christ. Before the mission was over, there was not a grown-up scholar in that Sunday-school, either youth or maiden, who had not followed her example. The last I heard of her was from her brother, who met me in London and told me that leading his sister to Christ was one of the best things I had ever been able to do for my Lord.

CHAPTER XV.

The Romance of Evangelism. (i.)

ROMANCE in evangelism? Yes, in *all* Christian work, and *most of all in revivals!* No boredom or ennui here, and no dead levels of monotony. There is *always* some kind of healthy excitement in the work; but it comes in so many different forms and ways, and the habits of retirement alone with God—referred to in a previous chapter—keep it so sweet and fresh that it never wearies but is always welcome. The perfunctory failures, and the cold lazy unsaved excuse-mongers in the churches, are fond of coupling *evangelism* with *excitement*, and the charge is *blessedly true.* There *is* excitement in revivals, and cold flat featureless affairs they would be if there was none.

But that is not a fault, nor does it supply the faintest reason for shirking such work. If we condemn and refuse everything that holds excitement, what shall we have left that is worth keeping? There are times of special excitement in love, in the home, silent prayer and quiet reverent methods all minister to and deepen the sacred hush in the meetings.

But through and underneath it all there is a pure excitement, a joyous fervour, a holy glad enthusiasm. And sometimes it breaks out in ways that bring holy laughter or tears of joy, or both at the same time. Some good Christians remember and bring up to date the old-time Divine instructions about "no axe or hammer or tool of iron" having to make a noise in building the walls of the temple. The answer to that is as unnecessary as it is easy, but certainly there is no prohibition of that sort for these days *in the quarry*, where the blasting has to be done and the stones got out and dressed. Most evangelistic work is in the quarry, and there we sometimes hear an explosion, see a wedge driven or a mallet fall on a chisel, and sometimes therefore see the stones and chips fly in a delightful shower.

However still and hushed the listening while we preach, and however easy to hear the clock tick during silent prayer, the holy glow is there, and when it finds expression it is generally "good to be there." Again and again when some one specially needing Christ and specially prayed for has started for the inquiry-room, or when a long string of fine young men, or from fifty to a hundred seekers of both sexes have gone in the same direction, I have heard expressions of joy and praise that must have been music to the angels of God. Again and again I have seen an inquiry-room moved with delightful excitement when husband and wife have risen from their knees and given each other the first kiss in Christ, or when four or five from one family have all found peace, embraced each other, and rejoiced and wept together. Only last Sunday week—December 3rd, 1905—I paid a re-visit to Darlington Street, Wolverhampton. All that crowded audience, except about a dozen, stayed to the after-meeting. A brief appeal and one prayer were followed by seventy-seven men and women coming out grandly for Christ. More than forty of these were young men. Man and wife came hand in hand, and in several cases there were among them several members of the same family. There was a joy of excitement both in the church and in the room, and who will dare to condemn it? "Evanescent," says the church cynic. I answer, "*How that*, when a string of those pointing the others to Christ were people converted in my mission there just three years before?"

How we pity non-working church members! How sorry we are for those of them who have not enough saving grace to give them saving sympathies! And the Lord Himself have mercy on the sneering cynical church critic! It takes fewer brains to set up a man in that business than any other of which I know, and the church critic of saving work is the smallest and most pitiful of them all. How much these poor souls miss and lose! How great is their close of the sermon I saw that he was under conviction and counting the cost of a full decision for Christ There are some timid ones who may be helped by a kindly word from some one near to them, but I saw that in this case such an offer would not be welcome, so I warned off an officious worker who was making for him. I saw the jaw set and the eye flash, and then the deliberate walk into the vestry, followed by the calm logical seeing of the truth. That man too is to-day a gifted and successful local preacher, the managing director of a large and successful business, and my happy helpful host when I mission and preach in his town. Every man by his own door, so long as he gets in. These two men were equally moved and excited too, but there was a mighty difference in their ways of expressing their feelings, though the result was the same in each case.

There are three words which together fairly summarize the various forms in which the romance of revivals is manifested; *the amusing*, *the joyous*, and *the sad*. It may be well to glance at the latter just here, and to reserve the other two for the next chapter. That tragedy and excitement may be closely connected some of us know only too well, and the romance of Christian toil has its own pathetic phases, and its joy is often splashed with tears. The nearer we live to Christ, the more fully we share, not only in the peace and joy He gives to His loved ones, but also in "the fellowship of His sufferings." We cannot bless others without being blessed ourselves, neither can we bless others without its costing us something in one way or another; and often, amid the joy of saving men, "the virtue has gone out of us" by the way of pain and tears.

If no one knows more of the joy of saving than a missioner, no one perhaps knows more of the heart-ache of "the unbelieved report," of the agony of the "unrevealed arm." Preaching to the same people night by night and hearing about them day by day, we get to know a number of faces, cases and personal histories. Many of these poor souls are in such peril or need that we give them a special place in our prayers during the mission; and I want to say now to the glory of God and to strengthen the faith of my readers, that *hundreds of my own prayers for individuals* in my audiences *have had prompt and glorious answers; hundreds of the requests* for prayer read out night after night *have had similar* answers; and one of my special joys is that in all these years in mission work, in nine out of ten of my homes, God has given me for Jesus the unsaved grown-up sons and daughters, and in most cases the unsaved servants too.

But all through those years there have been others over whom we could not rejoice, but sorrow even unto tears. Night after night they have come and felt the power of God, but resisted it, till the mission, with its special opportunities, has gone by.

now they are both heartless, godless worldlings. His parents have been nearly broken-hearted over the man, and my own joy over that man's conversion and early promise has been the measure of my disappointment and pain at his fall.

One other source of the sorrow which forms part of the romance of our work is *the early cutting off* by death of some of the most promising fruits of our toil. The darling laddie we have just lost was my own son in the gospel as well as in the flesh. Since he left us without the chance of a good-bye, fathers have told me how his companionship and witness for Christ led their sons from the love of worldly pleasure to the love of Christ. Several young men, joining the church, have ascribed their conversion to his words and influence, and mothers have told my wife how sure they were that their sons were all right when they were with our boy. Yet his life-work has closed before he was eighteen. "Taken away from the evil to come" is the only reason of which we are sure now, but God knows of other answers to the great "Why?" of our sore hearts, and He will give those answers to us "hereafter" and show us that His way was the best. And I think now of many a fine young fellow and grand girl saved in my meetings, who began a noble Christian witness and work at once, but whose life-work was closed while it was yet morning.

One of the sweetest watering-place missions I

ever had was in Folkestone. Our church is little more than two miles from Shorncliffe camp, and a lot of soldiers attended all the meetings. Every time the inquiry-room was opened there were soldiers among the inquirers. As at Portsmouth, Devonport, Aldershot, Dublin, Cork and other garrison towns, it was lovely night after night to see the fine fellows in uniform leading and pointing their comrades to Christ. Then came the South African war, and one of those converts conducted meetings and helped men to Christ all through that long campaign. It rejoiced me to hear this, but sorrow came even with such tidings of joy. Four of the dear fellows converted in that one mission were killed in the disaster on Spion Kop.

Our Lord had "the joy set before Him," and we His co-workers share in and help to increase it, thank God! But as He had pain and sorrow unto tears in His mission, so have we who in His name and power carry on His work. The pain we feel for those who refuse and those who leave Him is sweetened by the knowledge that even concerning them "we are unto God a sweet savour of Christ." Our sorrow for those converts who are early called from toil to rest is sweetened by the thought that such "weeping endures" only "for the night" and "joy cometh in the morning." And *that morning* of reunion with our King, and with those for whom we now weep, will rest at noon and darken unto no night of parting pain or tears.

CHAPTER XVI.

The Romance of Evangelism. (ii.)

THAT an *amusing* element is sometimes found among the expressions of religious feeling is not the slightest evidence of irreverence. When the Lord made the first man He put an element of humour in him as well as the other constituents of human character, and humour is no sin when rightly felt and used. To be amused at what is amusing is not irreverent either, for laughter may be as holy as tears, and very often the two are but the two sides of the one emotion. In many cases laughter and tears are nearer to each other than some people think. The house of God is the fireside of the children of God, and while not forgetting the difference between Him and us, surely we may there have *home freedom* and cheer. George MacDonald was quite right in claiming that "it is the heart that is not yet sure of its God that is afraid to laugh in His presence."

I have heard prayers again and again that, to the ears of the thoughtless critic and ignorant slave of a false propriety, would have been shockingly irreverent, but that were of God and well-pleasing to Him. It is the meaning, the intent, the desire of the heart upon which He looks, and not its verbal expression. Behind wrong words, or a wrong putting of them, He may see *the right spirit*, and answer the prayer, while thousands of eloquent and stately but soul-less petitions, fall before Him unheeded. I have scores of times heard a whole company laugh at a child's petition to its mother, but her heart of love understood the request and was glad to hear and answer it. I have remembered those times too and been helped to patience by them, when I have heard untaught and ignorant but sincere young Christians say strange things in earnest prayers.

Sometimes of course I have heard prayers that were not of God; but thousands such are *read* every Sunday. I have heard real prayers too, so awkwardly expressed, and sometimes couched in words so utterly opposite to the thought of the heart, that I could not help but laugh even in the pulpit; prayers that I dare not put down on cold paper. One prayer that sent a ripple of sympathetic laughter through a Yorkshire mission room I will venture to give. I was in the circuit for the Sunday in my college days, and preached in this mission-room on the Saturday evening. In the prayer meeting a lad of sixteen took part who had been saved a year before in one of my meetings. He had induced his sister to accompany him to that meeting and was intensely anxious for her to be saved. In his prayer he said, "O Lord, save my sister, save her in this meeting now, I bet she'll get saved to-night, Lord." Aye, and she did, too, for the Lord knew that was the lad's way of uttering the deep intercession of his soul.

But it is usually into amusing sayings that the comedy of evangelism finds its way. In one of my small town missions a young fellow got converted who had lived a sad life. He had been both in reformatory and jail, and his life-chances were poor and few. He had, too, been more sinned against than sinning. He slept in a back room at a public-house, and earned a precarious living by doing odd jobs when he could get them. The day following his decision for Christ, a middle-aged woman came to see me about him, and said: "My husband and I have been to chapel nearly every night, and last night we could hardly sleep for thinking about that poor lad C——. He can never keep his religion if he stops at that pub. If some of you Wesleyans will find him some work I'll find him a home, and wash him and tatie (potato) him and bed him for three shilling a week."

Bless the dear woman! My host and I could not help laughing at her, but we saw her kind solicitude. It was "fruit meet for repentance" and we were not a bit surprised when she and her husband both found the Saviour that very night.

In that same mission the son and daughter of a Methodist farmer were both saved and every unsaved servant about the place. Several of the ploughmen and byre-men were saved the last night but one, but the last among them refused. When, the next morning, his young master asked him why he had not decided with the rest the night before, he said, "Well mester, you know it was this way; my wife couldn't get to the meeting last night, and I were not going to be saved wi'out her. We were *married together*, we live together, and we are going to be saved together to-night." The dear fellow did not see that they could not have been *married separately* to each other, but he knew what he meant. When he and his wife reached the chapel early that night, they passed by all pews and sat down on the cushion of the communion, close to the band-room door. They were the first to enter the inquiry-room that night, and they were indeed "saved together."

Though there was a pitiful side to it, a very amusing incident occurred during a mission conducted by one of my colleagues in a small Lancashire town. One night a regular scapegrace, a confirmed street loafer, entered the inquiry-room. He was so utterly out of touch with anything Christian that one of the officials on seeing him enter the room said, "Why ——! Are you here?" "Aye," he said, "ah've been christened an ah've been vaccinated, but they neither tuk, so ah thowt it wur time summat wur done." What brought the poor fellow into that room we need not inquire, and how much he felt of conviction of sin we do not need to be told, but his view of matters upset the gravity of all who heard it expressed.

In one of my missions in the Midlands we had a grand victory, and scores each night were seeking the Lord. One night during the second week, when we were just starting the after-meeting, I saw the decent simple-minded young man who blew the organ come out of his place and look with a reckoning gaze at the clock. Then he made a bolt for the inquiry-room, trusted Jesus, and got back just as the second man I had called upon closed his prayer. I saw by his first look that he was wondering if he could get into the room, find peace, and get back into his place in time to blow for the next hymn, and he did too. I could not help laughing when at the close he came to me with a triumphant look on his face and "I managed it, sir, didn't I?" The same look and smile greet me as he comes in to hear me on my annual visit to that town.

In one of my earliest missions we were using the communion rail for seekers, and I was much puzzled by the conduct of a middle-aged man in the second centre pew from the front. I could see he was broken-hearted and sobbing, but he did not come out. When I went to his side he said he wanted to be saved and was willing, but he would not stir. Presently I looked at his boots and saw the reason. He mixed the plaster for some builders, and had come to the service in a pair of big ugly plaster-covered boots, and was ashamed to go to the front in them. I said to him, "Are those dirty boots your hindrance?" And his answer was, "Yes, sir, they are." "All right," I said, "put mine on to go forward in." When he saw me begin to unloose my boots and realised that I was willing to do this to help a stranger to Christ, he sprang to his feet, boots and all, and was soon kneeling with others seeking the Lord. But my little act of helpfulness so completely moved him that for two or three minutes he could do nothing but laugh and cry at the same time. Aye, and he made a lot of us who were near join him in both.

I close these illustrations of glad and holy comedy with an illustration of the density of the world about the saving motives of the church, coupled with touching self-sacrifice for Christ. One of the grandest missions I ever conducted was in a Northern town where most of the men are miners, railway men, or in railway works. The work of God so gripped the place that political meetings had to be given up and the publicans announced free coffee on the Saturday night, to entice the men to their premises. The official of a local football club could see that in the meetings something had taken hold of the best players in the team, and feared that if they got converted they would leave it,—which, thank the Lord! was exactly what happened. To avoid this, they sent the secretary to offer me—how generous!—*two guineas* if I would leave the town at once instead of staying for a second week. When told that I would not leave the town for *two hundred guineas*, his opened eyes and mouth made the resisting of laughter an utter impossibility. I sometimes wonder if the poor little Simon Magus has yet recovered from his shock.

In that town there were four colliers who owned jointly the champion coursing dog of the neighbourhood. They were all convicted of sin, and announced their intention of getting converted. They were at once offered five pounds for their dog, and at once refused. They had decided to be Christ's men, and knew that, if sold, the dog would help to confirm other men in the gambling. So they nobly sacrificed the five pounds by drowning the dog on the Saturday evening. The dear fellows loved the dog, and when they got back from drowning it their sobs and tears were most touching; but the sorrow was turned into joy when at the early prayer meeting the next morning the whole four found peace with God.

And now a few illustrations of the *joyous* expression of the romance of soul-winning. It is a joy that is sometimes uttered in shouts of gladness and praise, but, in my meetings at least, it is more often a joy that is touched with tender pathos and many tears.

Where would one find more joyous romance than in the following incident, part of which I gave in my "Sonship and Service" and repeat more fully here by special request? Corporal Spong, a young soldier in Chester barracks, found peace with God while I was preaching there at City Road, on the last Sunday in the June before the Boer war broke out. In the following autumn he was sent to the Cape with Buller's army and went safely through the campaign until he reached Spion Kop. In that fight he was struck in the left side by a Mauser bullet which passed through both lungs and made its exit under his arm. In the pain of his wound he rolled into a hollow in which he lay, missed by all the ambulance parties, *for three days and three nights.* At the end of that time an ambulance search party heard him as he sang hymns in his delirium, and took him to the hospital tent.

When the surgeons examined him they gave him four hours to live, but his work was not done, and he is living yet. When I got to Chester the following June I heard the story, and was told of the way the presence of God had cheered and upheld him in the lonely thirst and agony of those terrible three days and nights on Spion Kop. And I was told too that the story of it, given to the hospital nurse, had moved the city of Chester in a deep and tender fashion. At the close of my lecture that Monday night a young soldier came up the aisle and asked me to point him to Christ. When he had trusted and found peace, he told me that it was not only my sermon on Judas the night before, and my lecture that night, that had led him to decision. "You know," he said, "I have been with Spong, and I wanted the religion he has got."

In the following July I met a Church lady at Llandudno, who told me that Spong, when invalided home to Netley Hospital, was put into the ward to which she was a regular visitor. She closed her remarks to me by saying: "Mr. Waugh, he did me more good than I could do him, and I look upon him as one of the most remarkable young Christians I ever met."

Three weeks later, at the close of my Sunday evening service in the Grand Theatre at Blackpool, a man told me that his eldest son, one of my own converts, was one of the ambulance party who picked up Spong on Spion Kop. He also told me that again and again his son had spoken of the lad's faith and splendid testimony for Christ.

Since then, at Stockport, one of Spong's old schoolmates told me that a mutual friend of them both was in the same company as Spong when he returned to the Cape; also that his friend had written him to say that on the way back Spong had led ten of his comrades on the troopship to a definite decision for Christ. I saw the fine fellow a few months ago, and he told me he felt as well as if a piece of Boer lead had never been near him. He

Ruby and Willie Waugh.

worked splendidly for months at the Central Hall, Manchester, and he is now doing a fine saving work as a local preacher in a Lancashire circuit near Manchester. I shall be thankful all my life for having led that dear soldier-lad to Christ, and to the dear Lord who has kept and used him so well.

Sometimes the holy joy starts in the home and culminates in the church. On the second Sunday of a mission I held at N—— I preached on the Holy Spirit, and we had a time of melting power. After dinner a godly nurse, doing a fine work for Christ in the district, called for a chat with me. She told me that fourteen years before she and her three brothers had walked two miles through a pouring rain to hear me preach in Brunswick Chapel, Sheffield. Then, to my joy, she added, "We were all four converted to God that night, and my three brothers are now all local preachers."

When she had gone, a gentleman called to see me, who lived in a beautiful villa near to the church where I was working. His red eyes told me of his errand before I heard his words. He was in middle life, of godly parents, had a wife and family, had been under the gospel all his life, yet had never said "Yes" to the calls of God. He had been utterly cut up in that morning's service, and had come to me to be pointed to Christ. As soon as he had trusted and expressed his rest and peace, I said to him, "What about to-night?" His reply was, "No secret discipleship for me, Mr. Waugh; I am coming out to witness for my Lord."

When I made the appeal that night he held out his hand to his wife, who took it and was led by him into the inquiry-room. In a few minutes he came back to the pew and held out his hand to his two daughters, and they followed him into the room to join their mother in seeking Jesus. As I went into the room to address the inquirers, I met him coming out and told him I was just going to give an address to the inquirers. "I would like to hear it," he said, "but my work is not done yet. There are two young gentlemen friends of mine at the back there, I am sure they want to be saved and I am going for them." In a few minutes he brought them into the inquiry-room, and what a scene of joy we had to be sure! Saved himself at three p.m., and before nine he had led his wife, two daughters, and two friends to the same Saviour. In the whole list of its offered excitements, the Christless world can offer nothing so purely thrilling and exhilarating as that.

At the close of one of my sermons in a mission in Yorkshire, I saw three elderly people bow down for a little confab in the pew. When the appeal was made they all three came together into the inquiry-room, and three other married couples at the same time. At the back of the chapel in the centre sat two young mechanics, who worked at the same bench. One of them had prayed for the other for months, and had induced him to come to most of the mission services. When we rose to sing the last hymn he saw that his workmate could weep but not sing. He whispered to him, "Do you want to be saved, ——?" "I do that," he replied. "Would you like me to go up with you for company?" "Yes, please," was the answer, and they came into the inquiry-room together. Scores were there seeking Jesus, and all the workers had their hands full. The two just knelt down, and the saved man pointed his friend to Christ, and soon he trusted in Him and rejoiced.

Just as they rose to their feet one of the aforesaid elderly men left his knees, and the young fellow who had just led his workmate to Jesus said with a glad cry, "Father! you here?" "Aye lad," was the answer, "and I have got saved too," and he embraced his son with tears of joy. Just then the woman rose to her feet, and then came the cry, "Mother! you here too?" "Aye, my son," she said, "your father and I settled it that we would come out for Christ and be saved together," and she took her son in her arms and kissed him. And then the other man rose to his feet, and this time the man's cry was, "Uncle! you here too?" "Aye lad," he replied, "when Mr. Waugh finished his sermon, we settled it in the pew that we would all be saved together, and here we are, thank God!" I have seen a few things in these twenty-three years, but I have not often witnessed such a scene of glad and holy excitement as we had in that room that night.

I am writing this chapter at Buxton, and it is perhaps fitting that I should close it with an incident from the very last mission I conducted before coming here. It was a time of great and beautiful harvesting, especially among young men and young women. The youngest daughter of my host and hostess made a brave public decision for Christ on the first day of the mission. On the second Sunday their niece and her husband came to the house to tea, at which I met and had a few words with them, and then they went with the family to my service, while I prayed for them.

We had a glorious victory that night, and these young married people were among the very first to turn to God. After family prayers the elder daughter told me she was not right with God, but meant to be, as did her *fiancé*. Next morning, when she came down stairs, her face was shining, and she told me that in her room she had found peace through believing. When she met her unmarried brother, he said, "My word, L——! but you do look happy." She told him she was happy and the reason why, "but," added she, "I am coming out to-night at chapel to witness for Christ." To her delight he answered, "I will come out at the same time, for I want to be right too."

When the appeal was made that night, those three were among the first to press through the throng into the inquiry-room. A married son of my host, up in the gallery, saw his brother and sister and friend come, and with the tears in his eyes he took the same blessed step. As he passed me for the inquiry-room he gripped my hand and said with a sob, "It's me, Mr. Waugh! It's W——. I am coming to Christ too!"

What a scene of gladness there was in that vestry! By these four dear ones knelt a young married lady in deep spiritual distress. As soon as she saw the light she quietly passed to the side of her seeking husband, and showed him the way she had come into the trust and peace. An official seeing the tears in my eyes said, "You seem touched, Mr. Waugh." "Yes," I said, "here are three of my host's family who have just found the Lord, and I feel so thankful, because I have prayed for them so much." "Thank the Lord,' he said, "one of my sons has just been saved in the other room, and he is my fifth son saved in this mission." The man next him said, "Yes, and my three sons have all been saved too"; and then my cup was full.

The purest excitement on earth is the joy of a close walk with Christ. Next to that, there is no thrill, no excitement, so gladsome as what we see, hear, know and feel in this work of saving men. Aye, and the joy of a full assurance and the joy of saving are both *eternal*. Every cup of excitement that the world presents is at the latest stricken from